Page 1

1) 170	2) 1,266	3) 3,383	4) 11,500
5) 10,760	6) 11,943	7) 1,695	8) 22,389
9) 18,885	10) 109,536	11) 409	12) 160
13) 169	14) 14	15) 77	16) 1,054
17) 1,507	18) 21,743	19) 37,316	20) 26,217
21) 448	22) 518	23) 5,778	24) 8,530
25) 8,736	26) 1,050	27) 819	28) 29,323
29) 287,040	30) 336,798	31) 89,142	32) 194,472
33) 325,215	34) 861,678	35) 3,065,365	36) 87 R1
37) 715 R1	38) 10,226	39) 3,825 R5	40) 32,398 R4
41) 13	42) 63 R11	43) 746 R47	44) 1,187 R48
45) 2,335 R36	46) 4 R205	47) 47 R352	48) 67 R232
49) 248 R155	50) 612 R195		

Page 2

1) 120	2) 1,384	3) 5,519	4) 2,270
5) 42,936	6) 1,190	7) 11,506	8) 19,137
9) 140,332	10) 74,035	11) 657	12) 119
13) 52	14) 1,268	15) 1,656	16) 3,296
17) 5,962	18) 496	19) 51,737	20) 44,188
21) 3,910	22) 5,740	23) 2,176	24) 4,410
25) 2,379	26) 15,370	27) 23,994	28) 32,785
29) 97,196	30) 662,589	31) 22,790	32) 197,457
33) 515,524	34) 197,775	35) 183,057	36) 82 R4
37) 465 R1	38) 4,493 R5	39) 139,454	40) 114,271
41) 14 R46	42) 115 R28	43) 1,254 R1	44) 7,254
45) 22,854 R3	46) 3 R307	47) 130 R253	48) 188 R499
49) 765 R840	50) 1,144 R234		

1) 160	2) 97	3) 225	4) 1,049
5) 2,080	6) 1,465	7) 7,305	8) 11,652
9) 45,265	10) 44,163	11) 654	12) 79
13) 4,999	14) 3,416	15) 66,837	16) 20,313
17) 25,635	18) 115,915	19) 422	20) 683
21) 232	22) 2,576	23) 6,354	24) 18,750
25) 263,415	26) 3,953	27) 1,872	28) 12,300
29) 388,044	30) 2,486,016	31) 131,795	32) 705,528
33) 126,445	34) 1,402,770	35) 3,698,043	36) 52 R2
37) 145	38) 12,879	39) 6,840 R1	40) 101,328 R3
41) 56 R9	42) 129 R18	43) 1,365 R41	44) 943 R49
45) 14,542 R41	46) 8 R670	47) 106 R51	48) 309 R163
49) 153 R396	50) 880 R128		

1) 209	2) 274	3) 1,071	4) 1,904
5) 2,718	6) 13,293	7) 8,961	8) 8,793
9) 22,451	10) 17,598	11) 343	12) 614
13) 464	14) 6,999	15) 56,848	16) 40,746
17) 10,556	18) 52,155	19) 3,872	20) 27,888
21) 476	22) 1,770	23) 5,264	24) 35,132
25) 230,832	26) 3,591	27) 7,636	28) 58,800
29) 172,645	30) 1,623,092	31) 135,424	32) 737,715
33) 495,600	34) 486,638	35) 3,735,570	36) 112 R2
37) 344 R2	38) 13,107 R1	39) 2,877 R7	40) 143,316 R3
41) 28 R9	42) 68 R30	43) 1,173 R57	44) 595 R26
45) 19,335 R14	46) 11 R207	47) 353 R166	48) 38 R110
49) 654 R269	50) 1,867 R102		

1) 228	2) 229	3) 613	4) 1,034
5) 2,475	6) 9,382	7) 22,499	8) 1,647
9) 15,885	10) 19,160	11) 463	12) 3,892
13) 2,769	14) 47,685	15) 53,593	16) 16,154
17) 12,052	18) 339,666	19) 3,795	20) 21,354
21) 270	22) 2,768	23) 4,365	24) 28,378
25) 478,930	26) 1,634	27) 9,460	28) 11,286
29) 562,010	30) 4,546,412	31) 20,592	32) 15,035
33) 2,806,496	34) 6,830,784	35) 62,632,467	36) 64
37) 506 R6	38) 12,879	39) 12,330 R4	40) 107,940 R3
41) 5 R58	42) 120 R5	43) 639 R20	44) 871 R33
45) 6,680 R38	46) 16 R190	47) 832 R610	48) 82 R157
49) 141 R80	50) 1,103 R590		

1) Seventeen.

2) Forty-six.

3) Seventy-eight.

4) Two hundred sixty-four.

5) Three hundred eighty-five.

6) Seven hundred fifty-two.

7) Nine hundred ninety-four.

8) Six hundred twenty-five

9) Two hundred thirty-nine.

10) Four thousand, eight hundred twelve.

11) One thousand, eight hundred seventy-three.

12) Two thousand, nine hundred fifty-six.

13) Eight thousand, eight hundred eighty-eight.

14) Nine thousand, five.

15) Twenty-one thousand, eight hundred sixty-four.

16) Thirty-four thousand, eight hundred sixty-three

17) Two hundred forty-eight thousand, six hundred thirty-five.

18) Five hundred forty-three thousand, eight hundred fifty-six.

19) Two million, four hundred thirty-seven.

20) Seven million, seven hundred fourteen thousand, six hundred eighty-two.

21) Fifteen million, six hundred fifty-eight thousand, seven hundred forty-three.

22) Twenty-five million, seven hundred eighteen thousand, nine hundred forty-seven.

23) One hundred five million, two hundred eighty-four thousand, six hundred seventy-eight.

24) Six hundred sixteen million, six hundred sixteen thousand, six hundred sixteen.

25) Seven million, five thousand, eight.

26) Seven hundred nineteen thousand, sixty-eight.

27) Five million, eight hundred fifty-six thousand, four hundred forty-three.

28) Twenty-three million, four hundred sixty-seven thousand, two hundred thirty-eight.

29) Two hundred two thousand, four hundred eighty-seven.

30) Three hundred nineteen million, four hundred twenty-five thousand, two hundred thirty-seven.

31) Eleven thousand, two hundred ninety-four.

32) Fourteen million, two hundred forty-three thousand, three hundred thirty-three.

33) Three hundred twenty-eight million, two hundred nineteen thousand, three hundred ninety-six.

34) Four million, three hundred eighty thousand, four hundred fifty-six.

35) Forty-five million, two hundred ninety-eight thousand, two hundred seventy-three.

36) Six hundred eighty-nine thousand, four hundred seventy-eight.

37) Three billion, forty million, two hundred ninety-six.

38) Two billion, four hundred sixty-eight thousand.

39) Seventy-five million, four hundred sixty-five thousand, three hundred ninety-four.

40) Four hundred eighty-five million, three hundred nineteen thousand, two hundred forty-three.

41) Three million, two hundred sixty-five thousand, four hundred fifty.

42) Eighty-six billion, two hundred sixty-five million, three hundred ninety-eight thousand, five.

43) Four billion, two hundred forty-eight million, three hundred fifty-six thousand, two hundred seventy-nine.

44) Four billion, two hundred eighty-four million, three hundred forty-three thousand, ninety.

45) Twenty-three billion, two hundred thirty-five million, four hundred forty-six thousand, six hundred fifty-seven.

46) Three hundred eighty-four million, two hundred ninety-six thousand, four hundred forty-six.

47) Forty-three billion, two hundred ninety-five million, three hundred eighty-seven thousand, three hundred fifty-eight.

48) Three hundred fifteen billion, two hundred ninety-four million, five hundred seventy-four thousand, eighty.

49) Thirteen billion, four hundred eighty-three million, two hundred ninety-five thousand, four hundred forty.

50) Two billion, four hundred sixteen thousand, fifty-three.

Page 7

1) 60,000 62,000 61,600 61,580	2) 3,180,000 3,183,000 3,183,500 3,183,500	3) 2,020,000 2,016,000 2,015,600 2,015,640	4) 212,650,000 212,648,000 212,648,200 212,648,150
5) 31,590,000 31,589,000 31,589,200 31,589,160	6) 2,560,000 2,556,000 2,555,600 2,555,560	7) 30,610,000 30,607,000 30,607,100 30,607,090	8) 0 1,000 1,000 1,000
9) 61,460,000 61,459,000 61,459,200 61,459,150	10) 0 0 100 80	11) 615,720,000 615,716,000 615,715,800 615,715,830	12) 920,000 919,000 918,600 918,650
13) 60,000 61,000 61,500 61,460	14) 185,000,000 184,998,000 184,998,200 184,998,170	15) 78,190,000 78,189,000 78,189,200 78,189,190	16) 29,160,000 29,159,000 29,158,600 29,158,650
17) 220,000 219,000 218,600 218,640	18) 3,950,000 3,954,000 3,954,200 3,954,160	19) 718,170,000 718,172,000 718,171,900 718,171,910	20) 10,560,000 10,564,000 10,563,800 10,563,830
21) 4,990,000 4,991,000 4,991,500 4,991,500	22) 25,560,000 25,564,000 25,564,200 25,564,200	23) 71,810,000 71,814,000 71,814,300 71,814,350	24) 718,650,000 718,649,000 718,648,900 718,648,910
25) 2,960,000 2,961,000 2,961,500 2,961,480	26) 7,780,000 7,778,000 7,777,800 7,777,780	27) 8,190,000 8,195,000 8,194,700 8,194,690	28) 719,190,000 719,190,000 719,189,900 719,189,950
29) 221,220,000 221,221,000 221,221,200 221,221,220	30) 9,960,000 9,964,000 9,964,200 9,964,180	31) 12,350,000 12,346,000 12,345,700 12,345,680	32) 90,000 90,000 89,600 89,640

33) 2,620,000 2,619,000 2,618,900 2,618,940	34) 21,870,000 21,868,000 21,867,700 21,867,720	35) 2,210,000 2,213,000 2,212,600 2,212,640	36) 4,550,000 4,545,000 4,545,500 4,545,450
37) 70,000 72,000 71,900 71,940	38) 4,440,000 4,444,000 4,444,400 4,444,450	39) 48,700,000 48,700,000 48,699,600 48,699,620	40) 718,100,000 718,101,000 718,100,600 718,100,610
41) 6,150,000 6,155,000 6,154,600 6,154,560	42) 3,950,000 3,945,000 3,945,200 3,945,190	43) 2,915,860,000 2,915,864,000 2,915,864,200 2,915,864,180	44) 6,000,000 6,001,000 6,000,900 6,000,920
45) 30,000 30,000 29,700 29,740	46) 156,020,000 156,016,000 156,015,800 156,015,830	47) 17,800,000 17,802,000 17,801,800 17,801,820	48) 720,000 719,000 718,700 718,700
49) 21,630,000 21,635,000 21,634,800 21,634,820	50) 1,000,000,000 1,000,000,000 1,000,000,000 1,000,000,000		

Page 8

1) 40.7	2) 21.14	3) 48.4	4) 32.514
5) 34.4	6) 62.187	7) 42.1	8) 5.8
9) 2.86	10) 9.85	11) 2.52	12) 202.176
13) 240.786	14) 1.0014	15) 13.551	16) $66.26
17) $6.15	18) $19.37	19) $13.81	20) $56.18
21) .0246	22) 3.1328	23) .000255	24) 136.8
25) .004104	26) .03024	27) 9.88	28) 16.02
29) .15189	30) .2145	31) .000182	32) $2.90
33) $139.34	34) $22.75	35) $403.53	36) .0175
37) 1.75	38) 175	39) .014	40) 6.09
41) 4.4	42) .0002	43) 3060	44) 2000
45) .289625	46) .2005	47) 4800	48) 5.05
49) $500.31	50) $620.14		

1) 34.32	2) 37.4	3) 6.6	4) 17.07
5) 106.02	6) 31.37	7) 55.1	8) 46.2
9) 29.33	10) 21.09	11) 56.82	12) 9.3
13) 66.26	14) 101.9	15) 71.31	16) 65.1
17) 9.366	18) 50.29	19) $18.27	20) $100.52
21) 31.71	22) 1.972	23) 4.136	24) .4613
25) $3.75	26) 96.88	27) 351.55	28) .01872
29) .027472	30) $87.69	31) .000014	32) 309.52
33) .107	34) 53.3304	35) $282.35	36) 7.08
37) $32.62	38) 609	39) .0907	40) 9.03
41) 90,300	42) 75	43) .0005	44) 304,000
45) .0012	46) 1.5	47) .000026	48) $50.71
49) $306.07	50) $6,400.		

1) 40.6	2) 42.2	3) 33.4	4) 49.4
5) 41.48	6) 3.86	7) 7.586	8) 10.414
9) 4.2	10) 20.43	11) 18.92	12) 24.77
13) 23.71	14) 28.21	15) 2.129	16) 19.998
17) 31.07	18) $47.29	19) $8.93	20) $26.05
21) 19.352	22) .2138	23) .2295	24) .79443
25) .0036117	26) .00009	27) 100.56	28) 21.8463
29) .019	30) .00028	31) .42436	32) $28.65
33) $4.12	34) $ .52	35) $38.63	36) .802
37) 66.25	38) 750	39) .2515	40) .00204
41) 4,050	42) .003005	43) 6	44) .008
45) 14,125	46) 400.4	47) $122.27	48) $80.71
49) $782.00	50) $60,780.67		

1) 40.49	2) .03	3) 2.46	4) 18.07
5) 10.047	6) 6.6	7) 13.8	8) 22.85
9) 13.27	10) 22.6	11) 15.4	12) 946.54
13) 52.3	14) 60.76	15) 77.07	16) 86.97
17) 19.136	18) 4.086	19) .027	20) $940.20
21) .076	22) .476	23) .00243	24) 27.93
25) .20864	26) .24624	27) 7.44	28) .005045
29) .0001	30) 12.9206	31) 3.81	32) .0000624
33) $6.70	34) $ .67	35) $ .26	36) 244.5
37) 1,800	38) 180	39) 3.125	40) .006
41) 17.8875	42) 56.25	43) .025	44) .00125
45) 502,000	46) 5.07	47) 80,600	48) $6,040.
49) $50.31	50) $2,000.63		

1) 62.3	2) 72.2	3) 80.3	4) 70.4
5) 236.036	6) 14.064	7) 40.12	8) 24.64
9) 5.4	10) 12	11) 10.8	12) 17.4
13) 13.616	14) 93.27	15) 46.81	16) $19.30
17) $13	18) $19.93	19) $60.42	20) $25.25
21) .0021	22) .1596	23) 352.56	24) .027063
25) .0909	26) .009292	27) .13072	28) 1.83
29) .6525	30) .06255	31) .052074	32) .03913
33) $2.38	34) $1.92	35) $319.29	36) .06085
37) 6.09	38) 60,400	39) .0875	40) 2,000
41) .000012	42) 3,070	43) 31.25	44) .00004
45) 34.8	46) .025	47) 750	48) $377.75
49) $38.91	50) $148,737.50		

1) Eight tenths.

2) Seven hundredths.

3) Five thousandths.

4) Nine ten thousandths.

5) Two hundred thousandths.

6) three millionths.

7) Seventeen hundredths.

8) One hundred seven thousandths.

9) One thousand, seven ten thousandths.

10) Two hundred thirty-nine thousandths.

11) Five thousand, sixty-three hundred thousandths.

12) One thousand, one hundred eleven ten thousandths.

13) Three hundred forty thousand, one hundred forty-two millionths.

14) Four hundred ninety-six thousandths.

15) Eight hundred eight ten thousandths.

16) Three and two tenths.

17) Eight hundred eighty-eight and thirty-six hundredths.

18) Six thousand, one hundred forty and six hundred forty-one thousandths.

19) Twenty-five and four thousand, one hundred eighty-eight ten thousandths.

20) Six and ten thousand, six hundred forty-eight hundred thousandths.

21) Five hundred and five thousandths.

22) Five hundred five thousandths.

24) Eighty and thirty-nine hundredths.

23) Seven and three hundred sixteen thousand, four hundred ninety-one millionths.

26) Forty-eight and three tenths.

25) Fifty-six and nine thousand, one hundred fifty-six ten thousandths.

28) Eight hundred and one hundred forty thousand, eight millionths.

27) Four and five hundred thirty-eight hundred thousandths.

30) Seven hundred and seventy-three ten thousandths.

29) Seven hundred seventy-three ten thousandths.

32) Forty-six and two thousand, one hundred sixty-four ten thousandths.

31) One thousand, six hundred forty and six tenths.

34) Eight hundred eighteen and eighteen hundredths.

33) Seven and forty-seven thousand, eight hundred fifty-six hundred thousandths.

36) Three hundred seventy-eight and five hundred ninety-nine ten thousandths.

35) Eleven thousand, five hundred eighty-one and three hundred sixty-four thousandths.

38) Five hundred eighty and sixty-three hundredths.

37) Five hundred eighteen and sixty-four thousand, one hundred fifty-five hundred thousandths.

39) One hundred fifty-three thousand, eight hundred ninety-four and seven tenths.

41) Three hundred forty-eight and seven thousand, nine hundred ninety-five ten thousandths.

43) Sixty-one thousand, five hundred eighty-three and nine tenths.

45) Five hundred ninety-nine and nine hundred ninety-six thousandths.

47) Twenty-eight thousand, and twenty-eight thousandths.

49) Seventeen and three hundred forty-one thousand, eight hundred ninety-one millionths.

40) Seven hundred sixty-four and four hundred fifty-nine thousand, three hundred seventy-eight millionths.

42) Seventeen and thirty-seven thousand, two hundred ninety-eight hundred thousandths.

44) Four hundred ninety-one and four hunded forty-eight thousandths.

46) Forty-three and three thousand, six hundred forty-nine ten thousandths.

48) Forty-six thousand, eight hundred ninety-five and nine hundredths.

50) Seventy-four and sixty-one thousand, nine hundred eighty hundred thousandths.

Page 14

1)	50	2)	630	3)	80	4)	10
	47.		631.		83.		7.
	47.2		630.8		82.7		6.9
	47.18		630.79		82.71		6.90
	47.184		630.794		82.711		6.899

5)	670	6)	180	7)	100	8)	10
	675.		176.		99.		9.
	674.9		176.4		99.1		9.5
	674.94		176.38		99.09		9.47
	674.938		176.385		99.090		9.473

9)	110	10)	250	11)	0	12)	50
	109.		249.		5.		54.
	108.8		248.6		4.8		53.7
	108.77		248.64		4.82		53.68
	108.774		248.636		4.822		53.683

13)	270	14)	10	15)	4240	16)	990
	272.		8.		4240.		990.
	272.2		8.1		4239.6		989.9
	272.18		8.11		4239.61		989.90
	272.180		8.115		4239.615		989.899

17)	0	18)	700	19)	90	20)	90
	3.		700.		86.		90.
	2.8		699.8		86.5		90.1
	2.80		699.84		86.47		90.09
	2.799		699.844		86.473		90.091
21)	710	22)	500	23)	10	24)	90
	714.		504.		6.		86.
	714.1		503.8		6.1		85.7
	714.08		503.80		6.07		85.72
	714.081		503.796		6.072		85.720
25)	10	26)	450	27)	20	28)	700
	5.		454.		18		700.
	5.0		453.8		18.0		700.1
	5.00		453.80		18.00		700.05
	5.001		453.803		17.995		700.053
29)	900	30)	10	31)	40	32)	60
	896.		10.		38.		57.
	896.4		9.6		38.5		56.7
	896.38		9.58		38.48		56.66
	896.379		9.579		38.477		56.664
33)	340	34)	20	35)	90	36)	0
	343.		22.		88.		0
	342.8		21.6		87.9		.5
	342.79		21.56		87.88		.48
	342.794		21.556		87.878		.479
37)	70	38)	4780	39)	0	40)	80
	70.		4785.		5.		77.
	70.5		4784.9		4.9		76.6
	70.50		4784.88		4.94		76.58
	70.496		4784.884		4.940		76.585
41)	20	42)	600	43)	70	44)	60
	22		600.		72.		59.
	22.2		600.0		72.5		58.8
	22.23		600.01		72.49		58.77
	22.228		600.006		72.493		58.767
45)	90	46)	10	47)	350	48)	610
	95.		8.		347.		610.
	94.7		8.4		346.8		609.7
	94.72		8.43		346.81		609.74
	94.723		8.427		346.815		609.735
49)	0	50)	100				
	5		100.				
	4.7		100.0				
	4.68		100.00				
	4.679		100.000				

Page 15

1) 1 2/5	2) 1	3) 1 1/10	4) 1 17/60
5) 1 5/16	6) 1 1/36	7) 23/26	8) 1 13/20
9) 83/180	10) 23/40	11) 2/9	12) 1/3
13) 11/30	14) 17/36	15) 43/80	16) 23/56
17) 9/28	18) 17/30	19) 23/100	20) 7/12
21) 9/20	22) 45/56	23) 8/25	24) 9/56
25) 1/2	26) 27/100	27) 0	28) 1/6
29) 2/9	30) 17/40	31) 1	32) 1 1/7
33) 18/35	34) 1	35) 1/2	36) 4/7
37) 3/4	38) 19/27	39) 2/3	40) 10/21
41) 1 4/9	42) 1/4	43) 1 1/9	44) 1 5/24
45) 1 9/70	46) 16/81	47) 2/3	48) 243/560
49) 7/12	50) 5/8		

Page 16

1) 1 1/4	2) 1 7/18	3) 1 27/40	4) 1 11/60
5) 23/50	6) 13 1/140	7) 21	8) 71 1/63
9) 43 59/108	10) 83 23/72	11) 37/80	12) 27/56
13) 0	14) 13/55	15) 29/150	16) 8 5/6
17) 21 10/39	18) 4 25/36	19) 30 29/90	20) 105 25/144
21) 16/21	22) 2/3	23) 9/20	24) 45/182
25) 1/4	26) 10	27) 13 3/5	28) 21
29) 90	30) 16	31) 2 1/3	32) 1 1/9
33) 3 81/98	34) 63/65	35) 1 1/15	36) 10 1/2
37) 2 2/3	38) 8/9	39) 1 3/4	40) 7 7/9
41) 1 25/36	42) 2/15	43) 7 23/70	44) 8 7/24
45) 9 17/18	46) 3/40	47) 1 19/21	48) 945/1408
49) 6 8/15	50) 20 5/56		

1) 19/24	2) 17/18	3) 1 13/50	4) 12 5/12
5) 18 31/54	6) 14 6/35	7) 16 31/56	8) 18
9) 48 1/12	10) 66 2/15	11) 17/60	12) 0
13) 14/45	14) 2 13/24	15) 3 23/24	16) 5 5/13
17) 6 4/7	18) 25 57/88	19) 807 1/6	20) 69 13/36
21) 8/15	22) 3/16	23) 7/15	24) 11 3/7
25) 63	26) 45	27) 27 1/2	28) 45 1/2
29) 0	30) 36 4/21	31) 2 3/16	32) 49/80
33) 27/56	34) 7/8	35) 10 2/3	36) 6 2/3
37) 1 1/3	38) 2 20/23	39) 1 5/11	40) 1 17/24
41) 3/28	42) 3 1/30	43) 6 7/9	44) 14 1/5
45) 5/28	46) 1 11/14	47) 3	48) 104
49) 13	50) 0		

1) 1 3/10	2) 1 3/16	3) 19/36	4) 14 2/35
5) 17	6) 50 11/12	7) 441 41/48	8) 16 2/63
9) 90 31/140	10) 23 101/150	11) 2/9	12) 5/24
13) 10/27	14) 38 29/30	15) 56 8/63	16) 473 7/13
17) 91 15/28	18) 56 23/108	19) 11 13/24	20) 57 119/120
21) 7/25	22) 1/4	23) 27/44	24) 22
25) 41 2/3	26) 49 1/2	27) 0	28) 20
29) 68 17/21	30) 65 9/28	31) 35/54	32) 35/38
33) 1 7/20	34) 15/28	35) 2 4/7	36) 3 37/51
37) 3 19/52	38) 3 5/7	39) 13/16	40) 16 1/2
41) 1 157/168	42) 77/150	43) 4 5/6	44) 33 1/5
45) 91 31/42	46) 8 13/15	47) 7/52	48) 3 3/11
49) 11 7/88	50) 25 5/24		

1) 1 19/60	2) 27/56	3) 37/40	4) 11 47/144
5) 25 47/75	6) 100 17/60	7) 148 11/18	8) 13 109/132
9) 47 69/70	10) 114 53/56	11) 25/84	12) 101/168
13) 65/252	14) 5 1/3	15) 7 4/9	16) 121 9/91
17) 22 61/108	18) 5 35/78	19) 24 47/60	20) 429 7/60
21) 21/34	22) 66/133	23) 27/50	24) 10
25) 119 1/21	26) 45 1/3	27) 41 11/14	28) 404
29) 33	30) 36 11/15	31) 1 1/5	32) 1 22/63
33) 65/72	34) 2 2/3	35) 2 19/22	36) 1 31/47
37) 4 53/148	38) 0	39) 1 3/7	40) 77/96
41) 1 31/300	42) 5/24	43) 64/105	44) 73/90
45) 15 43/52	46) 9/20	47) 21/52	48) 3 57/296
49) 24 2/3	50) 16 32/45		

1) F	2) T	3) F	4) T	5) F	6) T	7) T	8) F
9) T	10) F	11) T	12) T	13) T	14) F	15) F	16) F
17) T	18) F	19) T	20) T	21) T	22) T	23) F	24) T
25) F	26) T	27) T	28) T	29) T	30) T	31) T	32) F
33) T	34) T	35) T	36) T	37) T	38) T	39) F	40) T
41) F	42) T	43) F	44) T	45) T	46) T	47) T	48) F
49) T	50) F						

1) F	2) F	3) F	4) T	5) T	6) T	7) T	8) F
9) T	10) T	11) T	12) F	13) F	14) F	15) T	16) T
17) F	18) T	19) T	20) T	21) T	22) T	23) T	24) F
25) F	26) T	27) T	28) F	29) T	30) F	31) T	32) T
33) F	34) T	35) T	36) F	37) T	38) F	39) T	40) T

Page 21 (cont.)

41) F   42) F   43) T   44) T   45) T   46) T   47) T   48) T

49) F   50) T

Page 22

1) 15   2) 45   3) 25   4) 15   5) 9   6) 4   7) 30   8) 5

9) 100   10) 14   11) 112   12) 37   13) 13   14) 81   15) 34   16) 5

17) 10   18) 135   19) 111   20) 66   21) 12   22) 8   23) 20   24) 144

25) 19   26) 24   27) 5   28) 21   29) 12   30) 540   31) 27   32) 10

33) 7   34) 400   35) 60   36) 54   37) 3   38) 230   39) 36   40) 108

41) 13   42) 161   43) 90   44) 20   45) 16   46) 100   47) 74   48) 10

49) 1   50) 210

Page 23

1) 10   2) 90   3) 9   4) 9

5) 46   6) 144   7) 45   8) 16

9) 30   10) 56   11) 23 8/27   12) 7 7/8

13) 16 2/3   14) 12 25/39   15) 22 2/3   16) 4 2/3

17) 6 2/9   18) 21   19) 3 11/50   20) 30

21) 20   22) 14 2/3   23) 1/4   24) 13 7/26

25) 121 1/2   26) 11 1/3   27) 84   28) 84

29) 16   30) 46 3/7   31) 8 21/25   32) 16 57/64

33) 92 13/17   34) 28 1/2   35) 51 9/16   36) 20

37) 3/500   38) 24   39) 72   40) 11 8/17

41) 18 3/8   42) 8   43) 21/50   44) 64 11/16

45) 3/4   46) 112 1/2   47) 106 2/3   48) 49/100

49) 26 2/3   50) 13 1/3

Page 24

1) 5/96   2) 3/40   3) 12   4) 3/7

5) 1   6) 1 1/4   7) 4/9   8) 1/2

9) 5/12	10) 5/8	11) 5/8	12) 1/20
13) 2 1/10	14) 2 1/12	15) 27/80	16) 1 23/25
17) 1/3	18) 1 2/3	19) 4/27	20) 1 103/140
21) 1 3/5	22) 1 9/16	23) 9/20	24) 1 41/120
25) 21/100	26) 1 3/5	27) 14 29/50	28) 21/50
29) 36	30) 1 5/13	31) 20	32) 1
33) 10 5/6	34) 34 2/3	35) 3 1/7	36) 3 18/25
37) 5 15/17	38) 1 3/4	39) 1	40) 1
41) 1/3	42) 1	43) 2 1/2	44) 1
45) 36 5/16	46) 16 1/14	47) 21 3/5	48) 1 21/23
49) 5 27/70	50) 33 1/3		

Page 25

1) 4	2) .009	3) 1.5	4) .112
5) .4	6) 1.08	7) 2.16	8) 30
9) 1.968	10) .175	11) .406	12) .00072
13) 8.1	14) 2,800	15) .175	16) .05
17) 20.75	18) .03	19) .216	20) 2.7
21) .4	22) .0003	23) .0256	24) 3.6
25) 6.4	26) .675	27) 115	28) 4
29) .08	30) .0231	31) .00365	32) .096
33) 9.344	34) .0768	35) .064	36) 6.65
37) 5.12	38) .064	39) 150	40) 2.68
41) 22.8	42) 10.65	43) 14	44) .645
45) 125.56	46) 123	47) 4.06124	48) 82.4
49) 15.26	50) 843		

Page 26

1) 39	2) 4	3) 18	4) 5

5) 12	6) .5	7) 90	8) .08
9) 160	10) .00048	11) 24	12) 168
13) 1	14) 24	15) 40	16) 24
17) 30	18) 160	19) .75	20) .015
21) 5/8	22) 20	23) 24	24) .012
25) .91	26) 18	27) 56	28) .003
29) 1.2	30) 3/4	31) 540	32) .08
33) .0075	34) 24	35) .45	36) .008
37) 1 1/2	38) $75	39) 1/9	40) 20
41) 3/4	42) 1,200	43) .126	44) $46.88
45) 2/3	46) .1	47) 16	48) 1/40
49) 1.2	50) 1		

Page 27

1) 35	2) 15	3) 126	4) 17
5) 5	6) 147	7) 22	8) 21
9) 10	10) 30	11) 11 2/3	12) 12 4/5
13) 48 16/33	14) 47 1/2	15) 54 2/5	16) 30 27/55
17) 25 12/17	18) 13 7/26	19) 14 2/5	20) 8 19/35
21) 3/8	22) 7/15	23) 1 13/15	24) 9 3/5
25) 3/17	26) 1 103/152	27) 1 17/33	28) 2 2/9
29) 21 13/22	30) 8 2/5	31) 7.6	32) 100
33) 46	34) 10.66	35) 1.9425	36) 14.7
37) 9.8	38) 50	39) .00288	40) .95
41) .75	42) .625	43) 8/15	44) 3/16
45) .3	46) 4.2	47) 7/27	48) .5625
59) 1 1/35	50) 3		

1) .5	2) .25	3) .75	4) .6
5) .375	6) .7	7) .07	8) .875
9) .35	10) .28	11) .625	12) .76
13) .14	14) .035	15) .9	16) .75
17) .4	18) .9	19) .75	20) .4
21) 1.8	22) .47	23) 4.25	24) 4.375
25) $.\overline{6}$	26) 1.2	27) $.\overline{428571}$	28) .75
29) 3.03	30) .006	31) 2.5	32) $.\overline{3}$
33) 4.4	34) $.8\overline{3}$	35) .8	36) 2.625
37) $.583\overline{3}$	38) $.\overline{81}$	39) 3.125	40) .48
41) 3.8	42) $.5\overline{3}$	43) 1.875	44) $4.\overline{27}$
45) .325	46) .0001	47) $4.\overline{3}$	48) .975
49) 1.07	50) 2.6875		

1) 25%	2) 50%	3) 75%	4) 33 1/3%
5) 66 2/3%	6) 20%	7) 16 2/3%	8) 12 1/2%
9) 60%	10) 30%	11) 15%	12) 37 1/2%
13) 83 1/3%	14) 62 1/2%	15) 80%	16) 87 1/2%
17) 85%	18) 34%	19) 70%	20) 4%
21) 95%	22) 52%	23) 42 1/2%	24) 22%
25) 84%	26) 110%	27) 55 5/9%	28) 250%
29) 63 7/11%	30) 80%	31) 230%	32) 75%
33) 101%	34) 290%	35) 75%	36) 3/4%
37) 60%	38) 14%	39) 566 2/3%	40) 375%
41) 92%	42) 460%	43) 60%	44) 100%
45) 8 1/2%	46) 5%	47) 675%	48) 60%
49) 60%	50) 171 3/7%		

1) 3/10	2) 3/100	3) 3/1000	4) 4/5
5) 2/25	6) 1/125	7) 1 3/10	8) 13/100
9) 131/1000	10) 12/25	11) 4 4/5	12) 6/125
13) 3/625	14) 4/25	15) 2/125	16) 1 3/5
17) 1/10	18) 1/4	19) 1/50	20) 3/4
21) 3/5	22) 3/20	23) 1 1/2	24) 3/200
25) 9/10	26) 9/100	27) 1/2	28) 1 11/20
29) 2 1/2	30) 23/25	31) 4 12/25	32) 1 3/1000
33) 3/125	34) 6/25	35) 3/1250	36) 2 2/5
37) 33/100	38) 67/100	39) 1 7/10	40) 17/100
41) 17/1000	42) 5 2/5	43) 5 1/4	44) 2/5
45) 1/25	46) 1/2500	47) 1/250	48) 25 9/25
49) 100 1/4	50) 3/16		

1) 2/3	2) 1/6	3) 1/3	4) 5/6
5) 5/9	6) 5/11	7) 17/99	8) 7/15
9) 6/11	10) 2/15	11) 6 2/9	12) 47/99
13) 7/30	14) 8 8/11	15) 5/12	16) 35/37
17) 77 7/9	18) 7/12	19) 4/45	20) 11/18
21) 13/33	22) 14/111	23) 2 7/18	24) 4 92/99
25) 1/300	26) 56/165	27) 6 13/90	28) 73/990
29) 5/333	30) 35/36	31) 39 5/33	32) 292/333
33) 202/495	34) 7 38/45	35) 133/198	36) 136/495
37) 127/333	38) 8 37/99	39) 33 4/9	40) 67/450
41) 376/909	42) 2066/4995	43) 91/220	44) 1241/3000
45) 4 136/999	46) 8 197/450	47) 2269/4950	48) 2 19/110
49) 761/9990	50) 2135/9999		

Page 32

1) 50%	2) 5%	3) 1400%	4) .5%
5) 30%	6) 3%	7) .3%	8) 40%
9) 4%	10) .4%	11) 140%	12) 14%
13) 104%	14) 1.4%	15) 64%	16) 640%
17) 6.4%	18) .64%	19) 110%	20) 1.1%
21) 70%	22) 7%	23) .7%	24) 10%
25) 45%	26) 100%	27) 80%	28) 8%
29) 180%	30) 18%	31) 1.8%	32) 11.8%
33) 118%	34) 67%	35) 35%	36) 350%
37) 3.5%	38) .35%	39) 920%	40) 92%
41) .92%	42) 200%	43) 20%	44) 202%
45) 20.2%	46) 703.5%	47) 13.1%	48) 4.55%
49) 290%	50) 2.9%		

Page 33

1) 1/2	2) 1/4	3) 1/10	4) 3/4
5) 1/5	6) 17/20	7) 9/25	8) 7/100
9) 7/10	10) 2/25	11) 4/5	12) 3/20
13) 1 1/2	14) 11/25	15) 3/5	16) 3/50
17) 3/500	18) 2/5	19) 1/25	20) 4
21) 1/250	22) 17/100	23) 1 7/10	24) 57/100
25) 39/50	26) 13/20	27) 13/25	28) 3/100
29) 3/10	30) 3	31) 3/1000	32) 18/25
33) 16/25	34) 19/20	35) 1/20	36) 9/10
37) 9/100	38) 1 9/10	39) 77/100	40) 77/1000
41) 1/3	42) 2/3	43) 1/8	44) 3/8
45) 1/6	46) 21/25	47) 8 2/5	48) 5/6
49) 7/8	50) 1 11/20		

1) .5	2) .05	3) .35	4) .03
5) .3	6) 3	7) .17	8) 1.7
9) .04	10) .4	11) 4	12) .06
13) .6	14) .006	15) 6	16) 1.5
17) .15	18) .015	19) .0015	20) .75
21) .075	22) .2	23) .02	24) .25
25) .8	26) .08	27) 1	28) .1
29) .01	30) .001	31) .45	32) .07
33) .9	34) .67	35) .035	36) .0035
37) .041	38) 1.75	39) .015	40) .625
41) .0375	42) .052	43) .0925	44) .1375
45) .158	46) .1925	47) .096	48) 1.2
49) 6.25	50) .13375		

1) .25; 25%	2) .5; 50%	3) .$\overline{6}$; 66 2/3%	4) .75; 75%
5) .375; 37 1/2%	6) .875; 87 1/2%	7) .55; 55%	8) .34; 34%
9) .07; 7%	10) .06; 6%	11) 1.8; 180%	12) .52; 52%
13) 3.07; 307%	14) .02; 2%	15) 1.4; 140%	16) .3; 30%
17) .03; 3%	18) 1.3; 130%	19) .003; .3%	20) 4.05; 405%
21) 9/10; 90%	22) 9/100; 9%	23) 4/5; 80%	24) 2/25; 8%
25) 1 4/5; 180%	26) 9/50; 18%	27) 9/500; 1.8%	28) 1 2/5; 140%
29) 7/50; 14%	30) 7/500; 1.4%	31) 7/10; 70%	32) 7/100; 7%
33) 1 7/100; 107%	34) 1 7/10; 170%	35) 17/1000; 1.7%	36) 3/5; .6
37) 3/50; .06	38) 3/500; .006	39) 1 4/25; 1.16	40) 4/25; .16
41) 2/125; .016	42) 1; 1	43) 12/25; .48	44) 3/25; .12
45) 17/20; .85	46) 19/20; .95	47) 1 1/5; 1.2	48) 4/5; .8
49) 2/25; .08	50) 1/125; .008		

1) .2; 20% 2) .28; ;28% 3) .25; 25% 4) 1.2; 120%

5) .005; .5% 6) .175; 17 1/2% 7) 4.25; 425% 8) 2; 200%

9) $\overline{.857142}$; 85 5/7% 10) $3.\overline{3}$; 333 1/3% 11) 1.125; 112 1/2% 12) $.\overline{63}$; 63 7/11%

13) .825; 82 1/2% 14) .75; 75% 15) $1.\overline{6}$; 166 2/3% 16) 2/5; 40%

17) 1/25; 4% 18) 1/250; .4% 19) 4 2/5; 440% 20) 4 1/25; 404%

21) 39/50; 78% 22) 39/500; 7.8% 23) 9/10; 90% 24) 9/100; 9%

25) 1 1/10; 110% 26) 11/1000; 1.1% 27) 11/100; 11% 28) 1; 100%

29) 1/125; .8% 30) 9/5000; .18% 31) 3/5; .6 32) 3/50; .06

33) 3/500; .006 34) 13/200; .065 35) 13/20; .65 36) 27/400; .0675

37) 67/100; .67 38) 1 4/5; 1.8 39) 1 3/20; 1.15 40) 23/200; .115

41) 9/80; .1125 42) 5/8; .625 43) 1/16; .0625 44) 6 1/4; 6.25

45) 3/5000; .0006 46) 3.125; 312 1/2% 47) 4 1/5; 420% 48) 3/400; .0075

49) 21/500; 4.2% 50) .0625; 6 1/4%

1) .25; 25% 2) .8; 80% 3) .5; 50% 4) .95; 95%

5) .3; 30% 6) .52; 52% 7) .65; 65% 8) .26; 26%

9) .375; 37 1/2% 10) 1.4; 140% 11) 1.8; 180% 12) $.8\overline{3}$; 83 1/3%

13) $\overline{.428571}$; 42 6/7% 14) .1; 10% 15) 1.1; 110% 16) 11/100; 11%

17) 17/20; 85% 18) 1/5; 20% 19) 1/50; 2% 20) 2 1/50; 202%

21) 11/25; 44% 22) 16/25; 64% 23) 1/25; 4% 24) 19/100; 19%

25) 1 9/10; 190% 26) 6/25; 24% 27) 3/5; 60% 28) 3/50; 6%

29) 1 3/5; 160% 30) 4/25; 16% 31) 9/100; .09 32) 9/10; .9

33) 3/4; .75 34) 3/25; .12 35) 1 1/5; 1.2 36) 7/100; .07

37) 7/10; .7 38) 7; 7 39) 17/100; .17 40) 1 7/10; 1.7

41) 7/20; .35 42) 17/50; .34 43) 17/20; .85 44) 1 1/2; 1.5

45) 3/20; .15 46) 1 17/50; 134% 47) 1; 1 48) $.\overline{27}$; 27 3/11%

49) 1 11/100; 111% 50) 7/200; .035

1) .5; 50%   2) .75; 75%   3) .35; 35%   4) .6; 60%

5) .34; 34%   6) .625; 62 1/2%   7) $.\overline{6}$; 66 2/3%   8) .74; 74%

9) $.1\overline{6}$; 16 2/3%   10) .125; 12 1/2%   11) 1.6; 160%   12) 2.25; 225%

13) .035; 3 1/2%   14) .05; 5%   15) $1.8\overline{3}$; 183 1/3%   16) 7/10; 70%

17) 7/100; 7%   18) 7/20; 35%   19) 3 1/2; 350%   20) 7/200; 3 1/2%

21) 9/10; 90%   22) 9/100; 9%   23) 1 9/10; 190%   24) 4/5; 80%

25) 2/25; 8%   26) 1/125; .8%   27) 1/10; 10%   28) 1/100; 1%

29) 1 1/100; 101%   30) 3/8; 37 1/2%   31) 3/100; .03   32) 3/10; .3

33) 9/20; .45   34) 2/25; .08   35) 11/20; .55   36) 2/5; .4

37) 1/25; .04   38) 1/250; .004   39) 4; 4   40) 1 1/4; 1.25

41) 1/8; .125   42) 18/25; .72   43) 59/100; .59   44) 1 2/5; 1.4

45) 7/50; .14   46) 3/100; 3%   47) 1.875; 187 1/2%   48) 19/20; .95

49) 1 1/10; 110%   50) 3.25; 325%

1) .2; 20%   2) $.\overline{3}$; 33 1/3%   3) .75; 75%   4) .9; 90%

5) .09; 9%   6) .009; .9%   7) .68; 68%   8) .85; 85%

9) .34; 34%   10) .625; 62 1/2%   11) 1.5; 150%   12) 1.75; 175%

13) .125; 12 1/2%   14) 3.6; 360%   15) $.8\overline{3}$; 83 1/3%   16) .08; 8%

17) 3.1; 310%   18) .31; 31%   19) .031; 3.1%   20) 5.023; 502.3%

21) 1/10; 10%   22) 1/100; 1%   23) 1/1000; .1%   24) 1; 100%

25) 12/25; 48%   26) 13/25; 52%   27) 3/50; 6%   28) 3/5; 60%

29) 1 1/5; 120%   30) 3/25; 12%   31) 3/250; 1.2%   32) 21/25; 84%

33) 21/250; 8.4%   34) 1 7/100; 107%   35) 1 7/1000; 100.7% 36) 1/5; .2

37) 1/50; .02   38) 2; 2   39) 2/5; .4   40) 3/4; .75

41) 23/25; .92   42) 18/125; .144   43) 21/200; .105   44) 1/4; .25

45) 2 1/2; 2.5   46) 1/40; .025   47) 2/25; .08   48) 4/5; .8

49) 1/8; .125   50) 47/400; .1175

1) 7/10; 70%   2) 3/4; .75   3) .06; 6%   4) 7/100; 7%

5) 3/5; .6   6) 7/25; 28%   7) .625; 62 1/2%   8) 1 3/10; 130%

9) .$\bar{5}$; 55 5/9%   10) 1 7/20; 1.35   11) 17/20; 85%   12) .$\bar{3}$; 33 1/3%

13) 4/25; 16%   14) 9/50; .18   15) .6; 60%   16) 1/25; .04

17) 7/500; 1.4%   18) .4375; 43 3/4%   19) 11/200; .055   20) 1 1/100; 101%

21) 21/400; .0525   22) .0175; 1 3/4%   23) 29/300; .09$\bar{6}$ 24) 17/100; 17%

25) 1.6; 160%   26) 5/8; .625   27) 7/8; 87 1/2%   28) .125; 12 1/2%

29) .4; 40%   30) 4/5; .8   31) 1.$\bar{6}$; 166 2/3%   32) 3 3/10; 330%

33) 1.26; 126%   34) 4;4   35) 137/1000; 13.7% 36) 51/400;.1275

37) 3.5; 350%   38) 141/1000; .141   39) 3/4; 75%   40) .375; 37 1/2%

41) 6/25; .24   42) 3/200; 1.5%   43) .4$\bar{6}$; 46 2/3%   44) 181/200;90.5%

45) 9/25; .36   46) .$\overline{45}$; 45 5/11%   47) 8/125; .064   48) 2/25; 8%

49) 49/500; .098   50) 1.875; 187 1/2%

1) 14   2) 475.2   3) 44.8   4) 35.75

5) 21.44   6) 66.3   7) 37.84   8) 81

9) 490   10) 433.26   11) 2.7   12) 5.76

13) 612   14) 3.61   15) 48   16) 5.59

17) 1,140   18) 3.2   19) 1.65   20) 7.5

21) 147   22) 11.05   23) .24   24) 79.74

25) 9.12   26) 196.1   27) 1.112.4   28) 275.44

29) 7.26   30) 43.4   31) 208.55   32) 2,250

33) 123.58   34) 375   35) 1,039.76   36) 38

37) 1.62   38) 215.18   39) 6.868.8   40) 24

41) 33.66   42) 2,897.55   43) 8.91   44) 710

45) 236.91   46) 4,712.5   47) 547.23   48) 369.63

49) 136.68   50) 1,225.26

1) 33.75	2) 78.75	3) 324	4) 11.83
5) 24.66	6) 38.44	7) 132.82	8) .25
9) 1,783.5	10) 203.28	11) 11.844	12) 3.456
13) 1.9	14) 8.134	15) .729	16) .088
17) .9024	18) 5.232	19) .3686	20) .1755
21) .0986	22) 81.75	23) .00884	24) .7344
25) 1.6	26) .374	27) 80.75	28) 18.844
29) 6.231	30) 3	31) 10	32) 2.5
33) 3.5625	34) 10.179	35) 11.3	36) 4.875
37) 5.025	38) .1	39) 1.39	40) 3.675
41) .062	42) 4.465	43) 2.759	44) 99.45
45) .00125	46) 2.3625	47) 104.25	48) 200
49) 20	50) 7/60		

1) 40%	2) 60%	3) 20%	4) 66%
5) 4%	6) 65%	7) 105%	8) 60%
9) 5%	10) 75%	11)120%	12) 52%
13) 8%	14) 68%	15) 80%	16) 25%
17) 75%	18) 150%	19) 37 1/2%	20) 5%
21) 75%	22) 75%	23) 75%	24) 75%
25) 75%	26) 40%	27) 5%	28) 25%
29) 80%	30) 22%	31) 40%	32) 380%
33) 40%	34) 90%	35) 5%	36) 40%
37) 80%	38) 125%	39) 5%	40) 1%
41) 40%	42) 160%	43) 12%	44) 625%
45) 15%	46) 40%	47) 82%	48) 3%
49) 75%	50) 40%		

1) 6.38	2) 266.4	3) 18.85	4) 4.86
5) 60.08	6) 100.74	7) 284.05	8) 94.09
9) 7.38	10) 962	11) 1.56	12) 1.232
13) 5.526	14) 5.384	15) 30.25	16) .0108
17) 1.44	18) 15.736	19) 2.346	20) .4185
21) .3528	22) .00196	23) 4.4588	24) .021
25) .2375	26) .836	27) .001665	28) .0378
29) .16	30) .02643	31) 6.125	32) 3.825
33) 1.18125	34) 1.05	35) .175	36) 46.238
37) 7.5	38) 3 29/64	39) .0625	40) 16 2/3
41) .0065625	42) .315	43) 2.4486	44) .45676
45) 3.45	46) 22.56	47) 20	48) 1/2
49) 713/750	50) 98		

1) 94%	2) 95%	3) 75%	4) 8%
5) 40%	6) 20%	7) 35%	8) 60%
9) 16%	10) 80%	11) 25%	12) 12.5%
13) 37.5%	14) 20%	15) 62.5%	16) 62.5%
17) 40%	18) 4%	19) 96%	20) 56%
21) 5.6%	22) .56%	23) 2.5%	24) 250%
25) 16 2/3%	26) 20%	27) 18.6%	28) 2.8%
29) 28%	30) .025%	31) 62.5%	32) 87.5%
33) 25%	34) 33 1/3%	35) 11 1/9%	36) 20%
37) 25%	38) 10%	39) 45%	40) 66 2/3%
41) 62.5%	42) 49%	43) 59%	44) 66 2/3%
45) 37.5%	46) 2/3%	47) 12.5%	48) 33 1/3%
49) 25%	50) 16 2/3%		

Page 46

1) 20%	2) 18%	3) 65%	4) 120%
5) 80%	6) 86%	7) 92%	8) 66 2/3%
9) 150%	10) 80%	11) 90%	12) 380%
13) 25%	14) 37.5%	15) 62.5%	16) 77 7/9%
17) 125%	18) 80%	19) 26%	20) 45%
21) 66 2/3%	22) 66 2/3%	23) 33 1/3%	24) 150%
25) 40%	26) 40%	27) 40%	28) 40%
29) 83 1/3%	30) 20%	31) 18.75%	32) 85 5/7%
33) 80%	34) 160%	35) 83 1/3%	36) 75%
37) 150%	38) 55 5/9%	39) 400%	40) 82%
41) 6 2/3%	42) 25%	43) 140%	44) 150%
45) 2.5%	46) 800%	47) 140%	48) 15%
49) 7.5%	50) .2%		

Page 47

1) 160	2) 375	3) 400	4) 2,000
5) 3,000	6) 162.5	7) 200	8) 186
9) 20,000	10) 80	11) 1,875	12) 300
13) 600	14) 8,800	15) 1,600	16) 1,700
17) 12	18) 300	19) 330	20) 25
21) 75	22) 87.5	23) 62.5	24) 300
25) 480	26) 1,280	27) 900	28) 133
29) 1,200	30) 400	31) 4,500	32) 2,000
33) 2,200	34) 36	35) 125	36) 300
37) 103	38) 2,500	39) 200	40) 7,000
41) 5,500	42) 8,800	43) 500	44) 1,000
45) 300	46) 300	47) 17,000	48) 900
49) 400	50) 30		

1) 400	2) 3,500	3) 200	4) 300
5) 400	6) 9	7) 6,900	8) 59
9) 300	10) 72	11) 544	12) 95
13) 5,600	14) 16,000	15) 87.5	16) 3,000
17) 60,000	18) 12,800	19) 30,000	20) 50
21) 2,000	22) 800	23) 2,000	24) 8
25) 40,000	26) 48	27) 46	28) 123
29) 200	30) 20,000	31) 1,000	32) 144,000
33) 675	34) 1,200	35) 1,500	36) 171
37) 600	38) 7,200	39) 1,600	40) 4,200
41) 2,400	42) 262.5	43) 1,000	44) 8,000
45) 12,500	46) 4,500	47) 1,500	48) 800
49) 3,200	50) 4,200		

1) 7,300	2) 1,800	3) 2,300	4) 7,100
5) 3,500	6) 16	7) 41	8) 89
9) 101	10) 5,600	11) 7,400	12) 66
13) 12,500	14) 46	15) 40	16) 999
17) 15	18) 31	19) 830,000	20) 357
21) 32	22) 634	23) 240,000	24) 41
25) 2.5	26) 302	27) 3,800	28) 62
29) 550	30) 421	31) 1,000	32) 71,000
33) 3,300	34) 1,200	35) 1,800	36) 1,800
37) 4,800	38) 3,200	39) 52,000	40) 98,000
41) 112,500	42) 3,500	43) 243	44) 210
45) 112.5	46) 4,500	47) 3,200	48) 4,800
49) 1,000	50) 100		

1) 30	2) 50%	3) 48	4) 45
5) 25%	6) 30	7) 35	8) 10%
9) 75	10) 108	11) 25%	12) 200
13) 255	14) 120	15) 75%	16) 48
17) 50%	18) 96	19) 60%	20) 144
21) 70	22) 25%	23) 25%	24) 96
25) 360	26) 75%	27) 25	28) 4
29) 144	30) 150%	31) 60	32) 60
33) 10%	34) 36	35) 128	36) 13
37) 40%	38) 75%	39) 16	40) $144.00
41) 60	42) 50%	43) $21.00	44) 20
45) 60	46) $250.00	47) 40%	48) 60
49) $15,000.00	50) 80%		

1) 40%	2) 18	3) 33 1/3	4) 25%
5) 65	6) 225	7) 33 1/3%	8) 70
9) 62	10) 35	11) 475	12) 52%
13) 65%	14) 350	15) 40	16) 350
17) 87 1/2%	18) 72	19) 40	20) 87 1/2%
21) 5.04	22) 13	23) 12 1/2%	24) 70
25) 300	26) 750	27) 6.25	28) 30
29) 75%	30) 62 1/2%	31) 540	32) 54
33) 40	34) 60%	35) 123.5	36) 65
37) 16 2/3%	38) 140	39) 83 1/3%	40) 5%
41) $6.60	42) 25%	43) 62 1/2%	44) $41.25
45) $412.50	46) $35.85	47) $136.00	48) 66 2/3%
49) $478.52	50) $5,100		

Page 52

1) 80	2) 37 1/2%	3) 25	4) 21
5) 65	6) 70	7) 99	8) 100
9) 52%	10) 135	11) 96	12) 26%
13) 240	14) 25%	15) 45	16) 85%
17) $16.25	18) 126	19) $141.75	20) 130%
21) 117	22) 12 1/2%	23) 56	24) $33.36
25) 33 1/3%	26) 200	27) $42.50	28) 12%
29) 300,000	30) $4,250	31) 65%	32) 22.5
33) $6	34) 30	35) 72	36) 3%
37) $52.50	38) $5.25	39) 6 1/2%	40) 1,500
41) 45	42) 65.6	43) 20%	44) $126
45) $357	46) .65%	47) 200	48) .6
49) 6 1/4%	50) $185		

Page 53

1) 50	2) 135	3) 75%	4) 23
5) 80%	6) 68	7) 64	8) 20%
9) 60	10) 40%	11) 100	12) 10
13) 25%	14) 32	15) 400%	16) $28.50
17) 6	18) $44.00	19) 25%	20) 40
21) $270.15	22) 50%	23) .35	24) 60%
25) $225.32	26) 30	27) 2	28) .6%
29) 4	30) 5.4	31) 70	32) $150
33) 12 1/2%	34) 128	35) 20	36) $155
37) 33 1/3%	38) 1 1/4	39) 83 1/3%	40) $2,740.5
41) 3,200	42) $7,153.50	43) 12 1/2%	44) $145
45) 37 1/2%	46) 51	47) $4.93	48) $64,000
49) 66 2/3%	50) $.64		

1) c   2) c   3) c   4) b   5) c   6) d   7) b   8) b

9) d   10) b   11) b   12) d   13) a   14) c   15) a   16) c

17) b   18) a   19) d   20) a   21) d   22) c   23) b   24) d

25) c

1) b   2) d   3) d   4) b   5) c   6) c   7) d   8) a

9) c   10) a   11) d   12) b   13) d   14) b   15) b   16) a

17) b   18) d   19) d   20) b   21) d   22) c   23) d   24) d

25) c

1) b   2) a   3) b   4) c   5) c   6) b   7) c   8) a

9) d   10) b   11) d   12) c   13) d   14) b   15) a   16) d

17) d   18) c   19) b   20) b   21) c   22) c   23) a   24) c

25) d

1) b   2) c   3) c   4) a   5) c   6) d   7) b   8) a

9) b   10) d   11) a   12) b   13) b   14) a   15) b   16) c

17) b   18) b   19) d   20) b   21) c   22) b   23) d   24) d

25) d

1) $30.63   2) $2.23   3) $15.22   4) $10.41

5) $19.47   6) $15.68   7) $7.77   8) $17.81

9) $ .60   10) $100.62   11) $28.51   12) $59.00

13) $61.49   14) $150.22   15) $17.36   16) $95.09

17) $9.22   18) $16.97   19) $11.05   20) $102.38

21) $2.49   22) $24.88   23) $ .25   24) $28.28

25) $75.00   26) $27.03   27) $ .31   28) $5.78

29) $ .09	30) $ .28	31) $ .68	32) $2.50
33) $51.43	34) $27.30	35) $6,909.26	36) $40.51
37) $16.18	38) $18.74	39) $137.61	40) $52.56
41) $30.02	42) $203.13	43) $3,057.14	44) $401.73
45) $501.59	46) $202.78	47) $310.62	48) $474.21
49) $1,002.00	50) $2,003,006.26		

Page 59

1) $21.60	2) $2.16	3) $1.72	4) $ .20
5) $5.39	6) $ .54	7) $2.12	8) $104.89
9) $.69	10) $2.55	11) $212.02	12) $538.59
13) $8.95	14) $415.67	15) $653.48	16) $22.95
17) $41.19	18) $601.32	19) $540.69	20) $771.28
21) $13.71	22) $63.02	23) $213.24	24) $7.90
25) $790.44	26) $8,082.50	27) $74.50	28) $6,120.67
29) $37,500	30) $102.08	31) $172.88	32) $5.07
33) $37.50	34) $2,857.14	35) $60.19	36) $781.14
37) $513.96	38) $476.19	39) $30.41	40) $800.00
41) $6.15	42) $410.00	43) $8.88	44) $29.82
45) $538.49	46) $2.00	47) $2,002.94	48) $381.84
49) $38.18	50) $20.23		

Page 60

1) $6.00	2) $1.83	3) $19.00	4) $38.85
5) $66.10	6) $31.00	7) $69.61	8) $57.63
9) $60.06	10) $84.36	11) $242.50	12) $175.00
13) $249.25	14) $68.27	15) $101.00	16) $69.76
17) $3.68	18) $21.06	19) $6.28	20) $ .96
21) $30.18	22) $3.02	23) $1,040.00	24) $216,000

Page 60 (cont.)

25) $113.00	26) $1.13	27) $180.14	28) $18.01
29) $4.45	30) $ .05	31) $16.05	32) $37.27
33) $1,515.40	34) $ .80	35) $47,500	36) $4.00
37) $5.92	38) $60.81	39) $7.56	40) $91.21
41) $30.32	42) $3.03	43) $27.21	44) $32.42
45) $91.89	46) $4.75	47) $217.50	48) $1,350.00
49) $44.69	50) $57.51		

Page 61

1) $23.52	2) $16.48	3) $13.00	4) $19.30
5) $19.93	6) $9.54	7) $11.00	8) $5.13
9) $40.54	10) $93.39	11) $4.25	12) $6.88
13) $9.16	14) $ .79	15) $32.50	16) $77.50
17) $1.00	18) $45.89	19) $11.10	20) $5.75
21) $37.75	22) $3.78	23) $ .38	24) $11.20
25) $ .32	26) $3.15	27) $67.50	28) $285.00
29) $12,000	30) $5.25	31) $15.06	32) $1,506.00
33) $8,000.00	34) $ .08	35) $906.11	36) $80.21
37) $6.02	38) $61,582.75	39) $ .05	40) $1,517.17
41) $47.50	42) $4.75	43) $ .48	44) $18.15
45) $1.82	46) $1.63	47) $20.40	48) $21.12
49) $45.54	50) $25.00		

Page 62

1) $20.00 $60.00	2) $9.00 $51.00	3) $2.55 $22.95	4) $8.80 $35.20
5) $3.25 $61.75	6) $2.80 $32.20	7) $2.40 $17.60	8) $18.75 $56.25
9) $4.80 $115.20	10) $700 $19,300	11) $3.64 $41.86	12) $3.00 $26.99

13) $4.63
    $13.87

14) $9.83
    $22.92

15) $4.99
    $19.96

16) $24.00
    $36.00

17) $27.88
    $27.87

18) $15.70
    $62.79

19) $4.24
    $56.26

20) $6.30
    $35.70

21) $9.50
    $85.50

22) $10.86
    $32.57

23) $57.00
    $543.00

24) $72.25
    $777.75

25) $68.00
    $782.00

26) $79.95
    $719.55

27) $15.99
    $63.96

28) $20.67
    $62.01

29) $2.07
    $39.33

30) $5.66
    $32.09

31) $954.00
    $6,996.00

32) $715.00
    $5,785.00

33) $1,440.00
    $5,760.00

34) $1,168.75
    $3,506.25

35) $750.00
    $6,750.00

36) $1,440.00
    $3,360.00

37) $350.00
    $6,650.00

38) $408.00
    $9,792.00

39) $1,224.00
    $14,076.00

40) $1,200.00
    $10,800.00

41) $2,250.00
    $12,750.00

42) $3.54
    $31.83

43) $5.22
    $59.99

44) $19.36
    $29.05

45) $24.21
    $24.20

46) $4.84
    $43.57

47) $7.35
    $29.40

48) $12.73
    $29.69

49) $1.27
    $41.15

50) $37.20
    $37.19

Page 63

1) $8.00
    $32.00

2) $15.00
    $45.00

3) $25.80
    $17.20

4) $5.20
    $46.80

5) $4.50
    $25.50

6) $9.00
    $36.00

7) $8.00
    $12.00

8) $12.00
    $68.00

9) $6.25
    $18.75

10) $8.64
    $20.16

11) 25%
    $30.00

12) 10%
    $45.00

13) 33 1/3%
    $40.00

14) 40%
    $27.00

15) 20%
    $24.00

16) 30%
    $52.50

17) 8%
    $82.80

18) 12%
    $396.00

19) 15%
    $6,162.50

20) 50%
    $24.27

21) 20%
    $12.00

22) 10%
    $4.00

23) 16%
    $8.00

24) 20%
    $15.00

25) 25%
    $14.00

26) 5%
    $1.50

27) 25%
    $36.00

28) 10%
    $7.55

29) 12% $9.60	30) 40% $18.30	31) $80.00 10%	32) $40.00 30%
33) $50.00 18%	34) $60.00 40%	35) $20.00 8%	36) $30.00 15%
37) $25.00 50%	38) $54.00 33 1/3%	39) $35.50 20%	40) $7,500.00 12%
41) $17.50 $32.50	42) 12 1/2% $126.00	43) $60.00 35%	44) 40% $180.00
45) $30.28 $45.42	46) 40% $22.34	47) $18.09 $102.51	48) $850.72 25%
49) 33 1/3% $240.00	50) 71 2/3% $4,300.00		

Page 64

1) $4.00	2) $15.00	3) $9.00	4) $3.25
5) $23.75	6) $17.50	7) $11.50	8) $36.00
9) $4.00	10) $18.00	11) $875.00	12) $660.60
13) $1,220.40	14) $327.25	15) $505.02	16) $399.96
17) $554.90	18) $191.97	19) $179.90	20) $532.45
21) $4,800.00	22) $6,600.00	23) $3,800.00	24) $4,530.00
25) $5,879.25	26) 25%	27) 10%	28) 40%
29) 13%	30) 4%	31) 5%	32) 2.5%
33) 10%	34) 6%	35) 12.5%	36) $85.00
37) $175.00	38) $640.00	39) $60.00	40) $98.00
41) $90,000.00	42) $40,000.00	43) $2,400.00	44) $500.00
45) $20,000.00	46) $425.00	47) $437.50	48) $83.99
49) 12.5%	50) $4,000.00		

Page 65

1) $40	2) $80	3) $146.25	4) $150
5) $36	6) $105	7) $2,700	8) $2,933.33
9) $3,420	10) $3,371.33	11) $588	12) $281.25

13) $720	14) $1,377	15) $1,296	16) $1,417.50
17) $200	18) $15,372	19) $3,000	20) $342
21) $765	22) $90,000	23) $99,000	24) $375,000
25) $270,000	26) $146,250	27) $159,300	28) $183,750
29) $97,200	30) $546,875	31) $57.75	32) $406.25
33) $87.50	34) $50.63	35) $125	36) $388
37) $900	38) $4,400	39) $962.50	40) $990
41) $82.50	42) $8	43) $32	44) $1,478.75
45) $1650	46) $1,495	47) $1,086.88	48) $1,728
49) $3,816	50) $987.65		

Page 66

1) $12.40	2) $8.09	3) $12.66	4) $25.15
5) $25.80	6) $35.00	7) $10.29	8) $3.83
9) $15.50	10) $18.80	11) $30.04	12) $2.41
13) $78.21	14) $225.00	15) $1,490.00	16) $7.57
17) $500.00	18) $71.18	19) $400.04	20) $47.50
21) $9.16	22) $5.26	23) $9.04	24) $4.01
25) $ .40	26) $600.00	27) $60.00	28) $20.68
29) $4.86	30) $7.92	31) $60.00	32) $79.58
33) $ .01	34) $620.00	35) $350.51	36) $84.00
37) $67.50	38) $47.50	39) $591.50	40) $4,110.00
41) $50.00	42) $120.00	43) $562.50	44) $600.00
45) $562.50	46) $11.25 $33.75	47) $6.60 $26.40	48) $40.00 360.00
49) $840.00 $4,760.00	50) $2,625.00 $22,375		

Page 67

1) $18.28	2) $21.72	3) $37.20	4) $2.21

5) $23.99   6) $27.00   7) $10.00   8) $2.57

9) $9.26   10) $84.30   11) $52.86   12) $4.53

13) $ .38   14) $57.06   15) $450.38   16) $40.50

17) $4,050   18) $120.51   19) $1,218.88 20) $1404.71

21) $72.00   22) $7.20   23) $54.00   24) $270.00

25) $540.00   26) $6.04   27) $3.30   28) $75.64

29) $30.31   30) $11,250.00 31) $ .95   32) $943.80

33) $237.63   34) $7,050.31 35) $7,125.00 36) $18.00

37) $76.59   38) $15.05   39) $5,070.00 40) $959.94

41) $112.00   42) $150.00   43) $275.00   44) $1,787.50

45) $281,250.00 46) $36.00   47) $2.30   48) $37.50
                    $108.00 $43.70 $212.50

49) $95.00   50) $30.20
     $380.00 $45.30

Page 68

1) −3   2) −12   3) −9   4) 11   5) −81   6) −21   7) 41   8) −82

9) 128   10) −209   11) 19   12) 64   13) −35   14) −84   15) −209   16) −286

17) −511   18) 791   19) −763   20) 0   21) 6   22) −12   23) 0   24) −17

25) −8   26) 1   27) 6   28) −3   29) 5   30) −4   31) 16   32) 5

33) −52   34) −6   35) −99   36) 117   37) −135   38) −28   39) −101   40) 213

41) 216   42) 28   43) 378   44) 110   45) −196   46) −267   47) −39   48) 728

49) −30   50) 0

Page 69

1) 1   2) −11   3) 4   4) 12   5) 43   6) −79   7) −77   8) 17

9) −32   10) 183   11) −400   12) 519   13) 251   14) 1136   15) −99   16) 294

17) 3230   18) 2199   19) −7516   20) −259   21) −45   22) 0   23) 48   24) −123

25) 59   26) 1739   27) −195   28) −9   29) −484   30) 572   31) 189   32) −245

33) 69   34) 169   35) −612   36) −588   37) −579   38) 396   39) 1254   40) −4086

41) 27   42) 222   43) −104   44) −572   45) 871   46) −236   47) −641   48) 387

49) 85   50) −632

Page 70

1) 2   2) −15   3) 12   4) −7   5) −12   6) 7   7) −2   8) 15

9) 11   10) −7   11) −23 12) 35   13) −11 14) −35 15) 23   16) 7

17) −84 18) −19 19) 23   20) −33 21) −7   22) −11 23) −86 24) −3

25) 116 26) 67   27) 18   28) −25 29) 0   30) 95   31) −54 32) 6

33) −28 34) −74 35) 7   36) 121 37) 7   38) 4   39) 77   40) −50

41) 1   42) 147 43) 0   44) 10   45) −173 46) 6   47) 55   48) 14

49) −70 50) 105

Page 71

1) −2   2) 4   3) −18   4) 22   5) 2   6) −22   7) −13   8) −4

9) 13   10) −6   11) −1   12) −36 13) 13   14) 6   15) −7   16) 36

17) −17 18) 30   19) 7   20) −49 21) −12 22) −26 23) 18   24) 48

25) −18 26) −16 27) 16   28) 6   29) −27 30) −10 31) 0   32) 26

33) −109 34) −32 35) 51   36) −51 37) −22 38) −42 39) 1   40) −11

41) 16   42) 17   43) −196 44) 77   45) 118 46) 76   47) −20 48) 22

49) 0   50) −10

Page 72

1) 27   2) 56   3) −45   4) −48   5) 50   6) −72   7) 49   8) 36

9) −88   10) −28 11) −162 12) 488 13) −252 14) 360 15) 158 16) 297

17)−5796 18)−1888 19) 1960 20) 2432 21) −48 22) 105 23) −270 24) −504

25) 192 26) −108 27) 126 28) 224 29) 81   30) −392 31) 672 32)−2268

33) 336 34) −840 35) 144 36)−1296 37) 105 38) 120 39) 320 40)−1120

41) −108 42) 960 43)−3125 44) −480 45) 960 46) 3780 47) 3888 48)−1440

49) 280 50)−6048

Page 73

1) −8   2) −12   3) −7   4) 4   5) 4   6) −15   7) −2   8) −3

9) 8   10) 2   11) −14   12) −30   13) −28   14) −20   15) 7   16) 1

17) −5   18) −10   19) 19   20) 6   21) 13   22) 5   23) −3   24) 3

25) 7   26) −3   27) −14   28) −15   29) 3   30) −3   31) 64   32) −80

33) −23   34) 75   35) −200 36) −4   37) 4   38) −20   39) 1   40) −1

41) 64   42) −1   43) 9   44) −12   45) −3   46) 6   47) 100   48) −8

49) 30   50) −45

Page 74

1) <   2) <   3) >   4) >   5) >   6) <   7) >   8) >

9) <   10) <   11) >   12) <   13) <   14) <   15) >   16) =

17) >   18) >   19) >   20) <   21) >   22) =   23) >   24) <

25) <   26) <   27) =   28) >   29) >   30) <

31) −7,−4,0,5   32) −4,−1,6,9   33) −8,−7,−2,−1   34) −8,−5,−4,6

35) −5,−1,0,7   36) −8,−5,5,14   37) −15,−11,−7,3 38) −8,−7,4,6

39) −6,−4,−3,5   40) −9,−5,9,14   41) −5,−3,3,5   42) −9,−3,3,9

43) −8,−3,4,12   44) −7,−5,−2,6   45) −12,−5,7,8   46) −8,−7,−2,3

47) −11,−1,0,21   48) −6,−4,−2,7   49) −4,−1,5,8   50) −6,−3,3,6

Page 75

1) −24   2) −12   3) 4   4) −9   5) −18   6) 0   7) 15   8) −20

9) −87   10) −44 11) 2   12) −14   13) 14   14) −2   15) −7   16) −5

17) −32 18) 21   19) 51   20) −119 21) −6   22) 1   23) 22   24) −28

25) 134 26) −48 27) −1   28) 68   29) −55 30) −177 31) −21 32) 6

33) 7   34) −21 35) 0   36) 9   37) −79 38) −38 39) −84 40) −50

41) 7   42) 5   43) −71 44) 50   45) 296 46) −20 47) 112 48) 12

49) −112 50) −34

Page 76

1) −72 2) −14 3) −8 4) −126 5) −72 6) 6 7) −8 8) −7

9) 72 10) 294 11) 8 12) 3 13) 240 14) 5 15) −6 16) −2

17) −680 18) 70 19) −29 20) 4 21) 120 22) −4 23) 5 24) 4

25) 432 26) 270 27) 3 28) 11 29) −432 30) 1800 31) −3 32) 5

33) −675 34) −8 35) 3 36) −450 37) −768 38) −1800 39) 3 40) 13

41) 480 42) −16 43) −648 44) −18000 45) −8 46) −20 47) 9 48) −27

49) −5 50) −400

Page 77

1) −4 2) −16 3) −18 4) 4 5) −10 6) 21 7) −18 8) −5

9) −2 10) −5 11) 3 12) 20 13) −13 14) 16 15) −23 16) −30

17) −4 18) 22 19) −231 20) 17 21) 48 22) −63 23) 60 24) −378

25) 225 26) −216 27) −1000 28) −504 29) −3000 30) −10584 31) 6 32) −12

33) −2 34) −1 35) 3 36) −8 37) −10 38) −10 39) 31 40) 2

41) −7 42) −9 43) 19 44) −20 45) 60 46) −8 47) −20 48) −640

49) 43 50) −9

Page 78

1) −14 2) −5 3) −8 4) 26 5) −13 6) −16 7) −46 8) −1

9) −20 10) 154 11) −5 12) −25 13) 39 14) −69 15) −10 16) −109

17) 6 18) −102 19) −48 20) 148 21) −56 22) 36 23) −15 24) 70

25) 60 26) −84 27) −135 28) −150 29) 144 30) 420 31) −8 32) 9

33) 12 34) −48 35) −20 36) 9 37) −4 38) 5 39) 1 40) 4

41) −21 42) −32 43) −28 44) 3 45) 12 46) 24 47) −8 48) 15

49) −16 50) 22

Page 79

1) 1/12 2) −1.7 3) 2 1/2 4) 6.4

5) −1 6) −2.78 7) −9 8) −17.96

9) 8 1/6 10) −5.9 11) −11 9/20 12) −1.85

Page 40

13) −5 4/7	14) −80.07	15) 11/24	16) −14.9
17) −14	18) −5.6	19) −1 29/30	20) 8.893
21) −2	22) −18.53	23) −1 17/20	24) 4.89
25) −22 3/4	26) 22.9	27) −2 5/8	28) −8.41
29) −6 5/6	30) −1.51	31) −10 19/40	32) −9.293
33) 7 5/12	34) −23.91	35) −2 11/18	36) 14.62
37) −1 23/42	38) −.071	39) −5 1/4	40) 17.811
41) −13 5/6	42) −11.358	43) −9 7/8	44) −39.25
45) 2.08	46) −20.015	47) −8.39	48) −8.289
49) .125	50) 1.815		

Page 80

1) 1 1/24	2) −3/8	3) −7/30	4) 1 2/3
5) 21/80	6) 25/32	7) −7/10	8) −17/72
9) −1 53/180	10) 1 5/78	11) −2 7/18	12) −11 2/3
13) 28 7/12	14) 49 9/20	15) 77 9/28	16) −11 5/8
17) −14 13/32	18) 3 86/135	19) −13 7/33	20) 1 17/60
21) 56 2/9	22) 6 3/7	23) −73 41/80	24) −41/48
25) −5 2/21	26) 6.71	27) −14.6	28) −4.48
29) 37.82	30) 1.81	31) −48.5	32) 277.86
33) −32.2	34) 64.556	35) 2.03	36) −50.5
37) −14.58	38) 1010.57	39) −178.07	40) −2.759
41) −4.62	42) 783.147	43) −13.06	44) −42.382
45) 919.97	46) .082	47) 28.8	48) −94.91
49) 83.28	50) −655.579		

Page 81

1) −7/10	2) 9/20	3) −1/20	4) 0
5) −4 1/5	6) 3/10	7) 1/4	8) −1/14

9) −5/36   10) −15 2/5   11) 10 1/2   12) 0

13) 30 1/3   14) −37 2/7   15) 33   16) −4

17) 0   18) 5 5/6   19) 34   20) −24 4/15

21) −2156   22) 34   23) −140   24) 0

25) −15 5/28   26) −10.81   27) 28.86   28) −761.4

29) .0288   30) −7.845   31) −.00036   32) 0

33) −446.4   34) −3.2048   35) −57.246   36) 299.796

37) −1.21765   38) −8247.2   39) 0   40) 3.4362

41) −2098.701   42) 13450.08   43) −78.6176   44) −631.3462

45) −82.656   46) 20.878   47) 21.7728   48) −3553.2

49) 12.62205   50) −3.18895

Page 82

1) 2 1/2   2) −.2   3) −5/8   4) 200

5) −1 1/8   6) −.16   7) 8/15   8) −16

9) 1/4   10) .2   11) 1   12) −.005

13) −36   14) −41   15) 15   16) −.05

17) −32   18) .05   19) 42 6/7   20) −1250

21) −72   22) −.01875   23) 1 1/5   24) .1875

25) 1/8   26) −1875   27) −5 1/3   28) −.3

29) −5/18   30) .04   31) 27   32) 4000

33) 1 1/2   34) −.00125   35) −1 1/3   36) −3.04

37) −198   38) .002   39) −3   40) −.015

41) 5   42) −.01   43) 40 1/2   44) 3/5

45) −72/125   46) −.18   47) 38.4   48) .075

49) 6 2/5   50) 5.4

Page 83

1) <   2) <   3) <   4) <   5) >   6) <   7) <   8) >

9) >   10) =   11) <   12) <   13) >   14) =   15) <   16) =

17) >   18) <   19) <   20) <   21) >   22) >   23) >   24) =

25) <   26) <   27) <   28) <   29) <   30) <

31) -1 1/4, -2/3,   32) -5/7, -5/9,   33) -1, -3/4,   34) 1/2, 2/3,
    4/5, 1 1/2   5/9, 5/7   0, 1 1/2   3/4, 4/5

35) -4/5, -3/4,   36) -1/3, -1/8,   37) -5/6, -8/10,   38) -4/9, -3/7,
    -2/3, -1/2   0, 1/4   2/5, 1 1/5   -2/5, -3/8

39) -2, -1 1/2,   40) -7/2, -1 1/2,   41) -4 1/4, -4,   42) -5 1/5, -5 1/10
    4/5, 1 1/3   -5/4, -5/6   -3 3/4, -3 1/3   -4 4/5, -4 3/4

43) -5/3, -5/4,   44) -3/5, 2 3/8,   45) -7 1/2, -3 3/4,   46) 4/18, 4/12,
    -1, -3/8   2 5/6, 3 1/4   3 3/4, 7 1/2   4/9, 4/7

47) -2/5, -3/8   48) -1, -4/5   49) -6 1/2, -6 1/4,   50) -7/3, -8/5,
    3/4, 5/3   0, 4/5   6 1/5, 6 1/3   -3/2, -5/4

1) >   2) <   3) >   4) >   5) <   6) =   7) <   8) >

9) >   10) <   11) <   12) >   13) >   14) <   15) >   16) >

17) =   18) >   19) <   20) <   21) >   22) <   23) <   24) >

25) <   26) >   27) >   28) >   29) <   30) =

31) -3.6, -3.59,   32) 7.37, 7.4,   33) -12, -9   34) -5, -2.8,
    3.59, 3.6   8, 8.7   -8.2, -5   0, 4.3

35) 2.47, 4.27,   36) -5, -4.9,   37) -1, -.81,   38) .935, .94,
    4.72, 7.24   -4.85, -4.8   -.18, -.09   1.03, 1.1

39) -7, -.7,   40) -3.9, -3.84,   41) 6.29, 6.3,   42) -4.1, -4.092,
    -.07, .07   -3.1, -3.09   6.305, 6.31   -4.09, -4.089

43) -1.5, -1.1,   44) 6.66, 6.7,   45) -5.2, -5.15,   46) -8, -7.9,
    0, .09   6.72, 6.752   -5, -4.6   -.8, -.79

47) .075, .08,   48) -2.38, -1.7,   49) -3.2, -3.101,   50) .09, .9,
    .8, .81   1.38, 1.7   -3.007, -3   .99, 9

1) <   2) <   3) <   4) <   5) >   6) <   7) <   8) >

9) <   10) >   11) =   12) <   13) <   14) =   15) >   16) <

17) <   18) >   19) >   20) >   21) >   22) <   23) >   24) <

Page 85 (cont.)

25) =   26) >   27) >   28) >   29) <   30) <

31) -1/2, -1/4, 32) -5/6, 0, 33) -4/3, -5/6, 34) -3/5, 1/2,
   1/4, 1/2   3/8, 1   -3/4, -5/8   5/8, 3/4

35) -6/5, -5/6, 36) -1.6, -.8, 37) -9, -.9, 38) -14.5, 0,
   8/9, 9/8   .8, 1.6   -.09, -.009   16.3, 20.38

39) -3.33, .333, 40) -1.6, -.111, 41) 1/2, .6, 42) -.75, -5/8,
   3.33, 33.3   .009, .238   3/4, .8   -1/2, -.3

43) -1.6, -1 1/2, 44) -15, .8, 45) .78, 9/10, 46) -1 2/3,-1.63,
   -.16, 0   23/25, 1.2   6/5, 1.3   1 3/4, 1.89

47) .66, 665/1000 48) -.75, - 1/2, 49) -8/9, -.8, 50) 1 3/5, 1.63,
   2/3, .67   3/4, .8   -5/7, -.7   16 1/4, 16.3

Page 86

1) .125   2) -.09375   3) $-.\overline{8}$ 4) .75

5) $-.5\overline{3}$ 6) .8   7) $-.08\overline{3}$ 8) .3125

9) $-2.\overline{6}$ 10) $-1.\overline{142857}$ 11) .2   12) $- .58\overline{3}$

13) $1.\overline{63}$ 14) 1.875   15) $-.\overline{6}$ 16) $-.8\overline{3}$

17) - .92   18) -.7   19) -.875   20) .6

21) -.625   22) $-.13\overline{8}$ 23) $.\overline{428571}$ 24) $-.\overline{90}$

25) .5625   26) -3/10   27) 303/1000   28) -3/5

29) 81/100   30) -143/1000   31) 2 3/5   32) -3 81/100

33) -41 1/5   34) 6 3/100   35) -783 3/5   36) 7 2287/2500

37) -4 1/5   38) 7 101001/500,000   39) -7 9/1000   40) 9 93/10,000

41) -2 183/200   42) 7 113/1000   43) - 14603/100,000   44) 263/1250

45) 57/40,000   46) 6 14183/100,000   47) 2 4143/10,000   48) -6 83/100

49) -13/25,000   50) 15 43/10,000

Page 87

1) -5/18   2) -1 13/24   3) -11/12   4) 57/70

5) -1 31/90   6) - 1/28   7) 2/63   8) -4 1/2

9) -1 1/4   10) -15 25/48   11) -8 43/44   12) -47/56

13) 1 37/50   14) -3 29/36   15) -18 8/9   16) 3 79/80

17) -1 194/245	18) -63 1/96	19) 10 7/120	20) 17 5/28
21) -4.18	22) -15.253	23) -18.46	24) 795.25
25) 68.53	26) -63.585	27) -7.6	28) 9
29) -87.7	30) 211.92	31) 77.53	32) -4.77
33) 63.51	34) -132.28	35) 441.715	36) 0
37) .712	38) -17.4	39) 113.31	40) -1.495
41) 1.975	42) -4	43) -.493	44) 0
45) -3.64	46) 4.77	47) -5.13	48) 1.53
49) 10.365	50) 2.87		

Page 88

1) - 2 2/3	2) -3 4/7	3) .89	4) -3.57
5) -6 1/4	6) -6.58	7) 1 19/24	8) 9.78
9) 12.19	10) 3 17/20	11) -77.9	12) 11 7/20
13) -3/5	14) 7.383	15) 4 2/5	16) 8.617
17) -3/5	18) -1.83	19) 1.82	20) -24 7/30
21) -10.78	22) -6 17/30	23) 1.82	24) 6 17/30
25) 6 7/9	26) -6.68	27) 24 1/9	28) 70.58
29) -1 2/5	30) -3.49	31) .18	32) -1 1/42
33) 22.6	34) 0	35) 2 1/4	36) -6.58
37) -11 65/72	38) 17.43	39) 1.577	40) -6 43/60
41) -1.08	42) 3.48	43) -.81	44) 0
45) 5.983	46) 11.29	47) 30.145	48) -3.63
49) 0	50) -.325		

Page 89

1) 1 5/8	2) -1/3	3) 1/15	4) -1 11/20
5) -1 5/18	6) -7/18	7) -1 7/15	8) -2/5
9) -9 1/6	10) 9 23/40	11) -7/20	12) 2 13/20

Page 89 (cont.)

13) 3 7/12   14) 6 17/30   15) −31/63   16) 11 3/20

17) 5 7/24   18) 0   19) −2 7/20   20) −6 7/72

21) 3.2   22) 5.75   23) 14.113   24) 3.5454

25) −3.143   26) −13.166   27) 27.178   28) −8.134

29) −1.5347   30) −63.63   31) −6.85   32) 7.585

33) −1.4   34) −18.098   35) 14.9911   36) 700.41

37) 5.11   38) −3.65   39) −1.568   40) −20.5241

41) 3.8   42) −16.325   43) 17.9   44) −9.55

45) 32.35   46) −6.6175   47) −5 5/6   48) 13 23/60

49) −.28   50) −9 3/4

Page 90

1) −5/27   2) −3 3/8   3) 3 3/35   4) −5/12

5) −7/20   6) −16/21   7) 4/63   8) 2 1/112

9) −2   10) 3 2/3   11) 28 1/2   12) 1 7/11

13) −136 1/8   14) −1 1/6   15) 13   16) −3 2/3

17) −25 1/5   18) −315   19) 7 27/37   20) −43 7/8

21) −10.478   22) 176   23) −.02   24) 326.65

25) −1826.78   26) −66.24   27) 1600   28) −10.2375

29) 5000   30) 287.04   31) −1762.5   32) −30.24

33) −54.36   34) −5205.2   35) 20.8   36) −72.45

37) .000204   38) −61.6875   39) −2.015   40) −1487.5

41) −10.625   42) 3.9   43) −37.61875   44) −19.114

45) −166.25   46) 288   47) −5175   48) 337.2

49) 72.36   50) 20

Page 91

1) 5/9   2) −5/8   3) −1/2   4) 1/6

5) −4/15   6) −8/9   7) 8/9   8) 5/19

Page 91 (cont.)

9) −2   10) −3 13/24   11) −1 13/27   12) −1 73/270

13) −48 3/5   14) 3 4/7   15) 16/35   16) −14/45

17) −16 1/5   18) −2 7/9   19) 4 1/4   20) −26 7/8

21) −4.98   22) 16.644   23) .023   24) −27.2

25) −10.179   26) −2.15   27) −42.5   28) .016

29) 5.7   30) 3.58   31) −7.5   32) 78

33) 44.8512   34) −80   35) −.000075   36) .0024

37) 18   38) −15.4   39) −.0124   40) .006

41) .140625   42) −180   43) −2 2/5   44) 16.5

45) −4 31/56   46) 5/24   47) −3.9   48) −40/147

49) −2 8/21   50) 11 7/18

Page 92

1) −7 8/15   2) −6.392   3) −5 3/8   4) 3.32

5) −13 22/35   6) 14.014   7) −20 5/18   8) 6.63

9) −2 19/24   10) −58.84   11) 31 1/2   12) −12.662

13) −.77095   14) 27   15) 301.29   16) 1 9/16

17) −.8   18) −9/10   19) −645.408   20) 2

21) −11.22   22) 1 7/20   23) −12.86   24) 8 13/16

25) −59.667   26) −8 17/30   27) 6.728   28) −6 23/48

29) 16.42   30) −97 13/30   31) −308.7   32) 490

33) −64.6272   34) 340   35) −240.40842   36) −6/29

37) −51   38) 108/175   39) 5.85   40) −1/25

41) 1 3/8   42) 8.15   43) −2 7/40   44) −26.06

45) 736.375   46) −12.474   47) −12.81   48) −81 1/4

49) −3.45   50) −1

Page 93

1) −16   2) −32   3) −192   4) −3

Page 93 (cont.)

5) −16   6) −3   7) −5.6   8) .3

9) .192   10) 5.6   11) 7.76   12) −2.48

13) 7 1/4   14) −10 2/3   15) −7 1/4   16) 6

17) 4   18) 11/12   19) .35   20) −.05

21) −1.05   22) .000245   23) 5/12   24) −1/4

25) 2 19/24   26) 8 1/18   27) −5000   28) −4.41

29) 5.256   30) .864   31) −7/8   32) 3/25

33) 3/8   34) 1/3   35) −.0625   36) −77.49

37) 3.6   38) −.005   39) 7 17/30   40) .2

41) .15   42) −.5   43) 31.075   44) −.54

45) 10.2   46) −6.075   47) 2.03   48) −270.165

49) −5788.8   50) 20

Page 94

1) 17.4   2) −1/12   3) 18.6   4) −1/2

5) −10.8   6) −1 5/12   7) −.3   8) −1 1/8

9) −.42   10) −1/12   11) 4.2   12) 1 1/8

13) .0108   14) −17/24   15) .03   16) −15/32

17) .9   18) −1 19/40   19) −.036   20) 1 1/8

21) −19.56   22) −2 2/3   23) 62500   24) 5 2/5

25) −3.39   26) −4 9/20   27) .0036   28) −10

29) 15.17   30) −19/20   31) −.0004   32) 1/2

33) −.11   34) 1 11/12   35) 1.62   36) −36

37) −34.96   38) −1 17/24   39) −16.$\overline{6}$ 40) −10

41) .35   42) 2 1/4   43) −8.45   44) 2.4

45) −1.44   46) −8.805   47) 47/60   48) 72

49) −1   50) 5.485

1) 8	2) 81	3) 1,000	4) 1
5) 1	6) 23	7) 49	8) 1,024
9) 256	10) 125	11) 243	12) 361
13) 27	14) 1,296	15) 4	16) 169
17) 1	18) 343	19) 1	20) 256
21) 810,000	22) 64	23) 1,000,000,000	24) 10
25) 1	26) 729	27) 2,187	28) 144
29) 32	30) 196	31) 100,000	32) 256
33) 6,561	34) 64	35) 15,625	36) 10,000
37) 225	38) 1,331	39) 625	40) 576
41) 100,000,000	42) 4,096	43) 1,000,000	44) 2,401
45) 2,197	46) 3,125	47) 8,000	48) 1,296
49) 531,441	50) 20,736		

1) 16	2) 9	3) 25	4) 512
5) 81	6) 1296	7) -256	8) -128
9) -243	10) 8	11) -64	12) -225
13) 81	14) -1	15) 441	16) 121
17) -49	18) 1,000,000	19) -7776	20) -100,000
21) 1/243	22) 1/729	23) 1/529	24) 1/125
25) 1/1024	26) 1/64	27) 1/576	28) 5
29) 36	30) 1	31) 32	32) 1/10,000,000
33) 144	34) 1/729	35) 27	36) 1/484
37) 8,000	38) 2,744	39) 1/59049	40) 169
41) 1/16	42) 1/64	43) 216	44) -1
45) -7	46) 729	47) -32,768	48) -1,728
49) -100	50) 1/14641		

1) 2^7 2) 3^{12} 3) 4^5 4) 5^{12}

5) 10^{20} 6) 6^{12} 7) 9^{23} 8) 8^{18}

9) 15^{12} 10) 20^{27} 11) 10^2 12) 10^8

13) 2^4 14) 3^9 15) 5^{12} 16) 8^{-4}

17) 7^{-6} 18) 9^{-7} 19) 20^7 20) 5^{-13}

21) 2^{12} 22) 3^{10} 23) 5^{24} 24) 4^9

25) 6^7 26) 8^0 27) 2^{16} 28) 7^{30}

29) 3^{24} 30) 16^{15} 31) 5^1 32) 6^6

33) 8^3 34) 9^{-4} 35) 10^0 36) 2^{-2}

37) 5^4 38) 2^{-1} 39) 4^1 40) 8^1

41) 2^{-4} 42) 3^{-9} 43) 5^{-15} 44) 6^{10}

45) 9^1 46) 4^5 47) 4^7 48) 6^6

49) 10^{20} 50) 9^2

Page 98

1) 4   2) 12   3) 9   4) 7   5) 15   6) 11   7) 6   8) 14

9) 17   10) 20   11) 13   12) 5   13) 100   14) 10   15) 8   16) 17

17) 19   18) 22   19) 23   20) 16   21) 18   22) 90   23) 29   24) 41

25) 39   26) 21   27) 96   28) 84   29) 26   30) 98   31) 95   32) 61

33) 57   34) 36   35) 87   36) 28   37) 46   38) 81   39) 99   40) 53

41) 74   42) 48   43) 79   44) 92   45) 44   46) 51   47) 77   48) 89

49) 31   50) 37

Page 99

1) 1.4   2) 4.1   3) 2.8   4) 5.2

5) 6.2   6) 7.1   7) 8.1   8) 8.7

9) 9.5   10) 10.2   11) 11.4   12) 12.2

13) 13.2   14) 14.1   15) 15.3   16) 1.41

17) 4.36   18) 3.16   19) 6.32   20) 7.21

1) 8.25   22) 9.06   23) 5.39   24) 10.39

5) 11.62   26) 12.49   27) 13.42   28) 14.32

9) 15.59   30) 16.28   31) 1.414   32) 4.472

3) 3.464   34) 5.745   35) 6.708   36) 7.483

7) 8.367   38) 9.220   39) 9.695   40) 10.954

1) 11.832   42) 12.767   43) 13.964   44) 14.526

5) 15.811   46) 16.823   47) 17.321   48) 17.748

9) 18.083   50) 18.493

) 4.25×10^4 2) 1.3×10^3 3) 8×10^5 4) 4.2×10^{-3}

) 9×10^{-5} 6) 3.2×10^{-2} 7) 6×10^2 8) 7.1×10^4

) 1.001×10^6 10) 5×10^{-3} 11) 1.02×10^{-4} 12) 2×10^{-2}

3) 6.5×10^5 14) 7.00001×10^6 15) 2.3×10^7 16) 1.845×10^1

7) 9.24003×10^2 18) 7.000007×10^3 19) 6.06×10^5 20) 9.99×10^4

1) 5×10^8 22) 7.5×10^{-4} 23) 6×10^{-7} 24) 5.9005×10^1

5) 9.2×10^4 26) 143,000   27) 600,000,000   28) 7,200

9) .00052   30) .00000875   31) .005   32) 67,540,000

3) 317,000   34) 81,000   35) .3   36) .0472

7) .00000751   38) 840,000   39) 555.5   40) 1,234,500

1) .000273   42) .000000815   43) .0006   44) 920

5) 65.2   46) 4.85   47) .002145   48) .0000032

9) .172   50) 483,200,000

) 3.5×10^7 2) 2.52×10^9 3) 1.7472×10^8 4) 1.19×10^5

) 4.5×10^{14} 6) 3.45×10^{-5} 7) 4.08×10^{10} 8) 2.1112×10^3

) 1.848×10^{11} 10) 1.2×10^8 11) 2.4×10^{12} 12) 4.371×10^{12}

3) 5.8×10^9 14) 1.26×10^{14} 15) 4.575×10^8 16) 2×10^2

Page 101 (cont.)

17) 4.3×10^3 18) 5×10^2 19) 1.06×10^7 20) 5×10^1

21) 4×10^0 22) 1.81×10^3 23) 4×10^{-4} 24) 1.608×10^2

25) 2×10^1 26) 2.4×10^1 27) 6×10^{-1} 28) 4.5×10^{11}

29) 9×10^{-10} 30) 1×10^{13}

Page 102

1) 32   2) 81   3) 125   4) 512

5) −343   6) 1/256   7) 1296   8) 729

9) 1,331   10) 144   11) 1/6561   12) −100,000

13) 1/64   14) 10,000,000   15) 49   16) 5^7

17) 6^6 18) 8^{-4} 19) 9^2 20) 19^{-3}

21) 25^1 22) 6^{12} 23) 8^{10} 24) 4^{-64}

25) 6^3 26) 7^5 27) 8^{-17} 28) $(-3)^{-5}$

29) $(-8)^{-6}$ 30) 4^{-9} 31) 3   32) 1.41

33) 9   34) 3.16   35) 36   36) 12.25

37) 11   38) 81   39) 9.22   40) 16.58

41) 3.95×10^8 42) 7.6543×10^7 43) 8×10^{-6} 44) 8.65×10^{-8}

45) 7×10^{13} 46) 1.6×10^7 47) 2.16×10^{-8} 48) 8.96×10^{12}

49) 3×10^5 50) 4×10^2

Page 103

1) 16 qts.   2) 5 qts.   3) 7 gals.   4) 72 pts.

5) 22 qts.   6) 8 gals.   7) 6 gals.   8) 48 qts.

9) 8 1/2 qts.   10) 48 oz.   11) 8,000 lbs.   12) 9 lbs.

13) 7 tons   14) 96,000 oz.   15) 15,840 ft.   16) 24 yds.

17) 8 ft.   18) 768 in.   19) 252 in.   20) 14,080 yds.

21) 6 miles   22) 14 yds.   23) 420 mins.   24) 7,200 mins.

25) 60 hrs.   26) 1,176 hrs.   27) 13 days   28) 172,800 secs.

29) 10,080 mins. 30) 450 mins.   31) 6 gals.   32) 7 lbs. 1 oz.

Page 103 (cont.)

33) 6 days 1 hr. 50 mins   34) 3 ft. 10 in.   35) 1 day 17 hrs. 55 mins

Page 104

1) 168 in.	2) 315 ft.	3) 72 miles	4) 211 yds.
5) 390,720 ft.	6) 304 ft.	7) 22,800 yds.	8) 26,064 ins.
9) 48 qts.	10) 31 qts.	11) 120 pts.	12) 8 gals.
13) 12 gals.	14) 42 pts.	15) 132 qts.	16) 28 qts.
17) 192 oz.	18) 24 lbs.	19) 12,000 lbs.	20) 22 tons
21) 64,000 oz.	22) 211 mins	23) 17 days	24) 133 days
25) 504 hrs.	26) 13 hrs.	27) 28,800 sec.	28) 8,640 mins.
29) 312 weeks	30) 2,016 hrs.	31) 26 lbs. 1 oz	32) 9 yds 2 ft. 1 in.

33) 5 days 17 hrs. 54 mins.   34) 9 gals. 2 qts.   35) 4 yds. 1 ft. 9 in.

Page 105

1) .0063 m	2) 8700 mm	3) 93000 cm	4) 80 km
5) 9472 mm	6) .03 dam	7) 91,300,000 mm	8) .00004 m
9) 79,140 cm	10) 21,400 mm	11) .0777 g	12) 82 dg
13) 94.2 g	14) .001 kg	15) 1,000,000 mg	16) 30,400 cg
17) 6.3 mg	18) 8,810 dg	19) .000034 kg	20) .8 dg
21) 170 dl	22) 93.5 ml	23) 111,000 L	24) .00851 dal
25) .000087 kl	26) .0147 kl	27) .9536 dal	28) 170 ml
29) .725 kl	30) 4,710,000 cl	31) 4,700 mm	32) 48,500 cl
33) .0842 g	34) .018 kl	35) .047 m	36) 8,000,000 mg
37) .93 dal	38) 410 hm	39) 324 dg	40) 80,000 cm
41) 93,000 L	42) 8.1 ML	43) .009414 hg	44) .064352 m
45) .0009 dag	46) .00137 hl	47) 430 cm	48) 145,000 mg
49) 1,430 dl	50) 8.875 km		

Page 106

1) .049 kg	2) .0073 dag	3) 8.25 dg	4) 950 cg

Page 106 (cont.)

5) .8725 kg 6) 40 mg 7) 14,200 cg 8) .92 g

9) .0376 dg 10) .09973 hg 11) 94 dl 12) .0042 cl

13) .8764 kl 14) .25 l 15) 48,500 ml 16) .274 cl

17) .881 dal 18) .3675 hl 19) 7,000,000 ml 20) .4 l

21) .00047 hm 22) .0097 km 23) 8,900 mm 24) 937 dm

25) 47,500 cm 26) .0984 dm 27) 27,600,000 cm 28) 460 mm

29) 48.52 cm 30) 95,800 mm 31) 8,700 mg 32) .045 l

33) 800,000 cm 34) 95,000 dl 35) .000467 hm 36) .0085 g

37) 41,500 cl 38) 9,300,000 mm 39) .0085 dag 40) 7,800 mm

41) .00000054 kl 42) .93 m 43) .000841 hl 44) 474 dg

45) 4.5 km 46) 840,000 cl 47) .073 dal 48) .00004 cm

49) 45,000 g 50) .0015 hl

Page 107

1) 64 cm, 240 cm^2 2) 52 in,160 in^2 3) 36 ft, 81 ft^2 4) 50 cm, 136 cm^2

5) 50 in, 150 in^2 6) 120 cm,900 cm^2 7) 66 ft,200 ft.^{2} 8) 56 m,180 m^2

9) 52 cm,169 cm^2 10) 74 in,210 in^2 11) 80 cm,336 cm^2 12) 110 yd,750 yd^2

13) 108 m,560 m^2 14) 140 cm,1225 cm^2 15) 116 ft,720 ft^2 16) 22 cm, 30 $^1/_4$ cm

17) 96 in,536.31 in^2 18) 10 ft,6.25 ft^2 19) 35 3/4 in,77 1/32 in^2

20) 66.2 ft., 257.5 ft^2 21) 70 cm, 300 cm^2 22) 100 cm, 525 cm^2

23) 160 yd, 1500 yd^2 24) 308 yd, 5,400 yd^2 25) 126 in, 950 in^2

26) 54 in, 162 in^2 27) 90 in, 500 in^2 28) 150 ft, 1350 t^2

29) 98 ft, 580 ft.^{2} 30) 21 2/3 m, 25 m^2 31) 25 1/5 m, 38 m^2

32) 28 cm, 47.31 cm^2 33) 4.6 km, .9 km^2 34) 9 km, 5 km^2

35) 100 cm, 625 cm^2 36) 160 cm, 1600 cm^2 37) 56 m, 196 m^2

38) 60 m, 225 m^2 39) 1000 ft, 62,500 ft^2 40) 500 ft, 15,625 ft^2

Page 108

1) 60 in, 150 in^2 2) 30 cm, 30 cm^2 3) 36m, 54 m^2

Page 108 (cont.)

4) 73 cm, 255 cm^2 5) 25 m, 25 m^2 6) 37 ft. 24 ft^2

7) 12 ft, 6 ft.^{2} 8) 40 in, 60 in^2 9) 48 m, 96 m^2

10) 60 in, 120 in^2 11) 80 ft, 240 ft^2 12) 180 m, 1350 m^2

13) 56 in, 84 in^2 14) 24 cm, 24 cm^2 15) 144 m, 864 m^2

16) 120 ft, 600 ft^2 17) 120 in, 540 in^2 18) 112 cm, 336 cm^2

19) 18ft, 13 1/2 ft^2 20) 9 cm, 2.7 cm^2 21) 64 in, 160 in^2

22) 105 cm, 437.5 cm^2 23) 43 cm, 65 cm^2 24) 67 m, 200 m^2

25) 76 ft, 225 ft^2 26) 62 in, 120 in^2 27) 115 cm, 500 cm^2

28) 235 cm, 1950 cm^2 29) 105 m, 270 m^2 30) 130 ft, 420 ft^2

31) 45 in, 90 in^2 32) 240 cm, 2600 cm^2 33) 120 ft, 750 ft^2

34) 135 m, 500 m^2 35) 105 in, 562.5 in^2 36) 58 ft, 80 ft^2

37) 54 cm, 126 cm^2 38) 60 m, 150 m^2 39) 40 1/30 cm, 62 1/2 cm^2

40) 47.3 ft, 73.525 ft^2

Page 109

1) 86 cm, 300 cm^2 2) 100 m, 500 m^2 3) 58 cm, 150 cm^2

4) 100 m, 450 m^2 5) 86 in, 375 in^2 6) 32 in, 40 in^2

7) 116 ft, 540 ft^2 8) 72 ft, 252 ft^2 9) 180 cm, 1600 cm^2

10) 120 cm, 660 cm^2 11) 78 cm, 250 cm^2 12) 144 cm, 960 cm^2

13) 34 km, 54 km^2 14) 88 in, 308 in^2 15) 98 in, 480 in^2

16) 80 ft, 300 ft^2 17) 200 in, 2000 in^2 18) 124 cm, 680 cm^2

19) 168 m, 1280 m^2 20) 53 ft, 116 ft^2 21) 70 in, 200 in^2

22) 69 cm, 240 cm^2 23) 50 in, 125 in^2 24) 106 in, 625 in^2

25) 95 cm, 470 cm^2 26) 110 cm, 600 cm^2 27) 92 ft, 384 ft^2

28) 105 ft, 550 ft^2 29) 145 ft, 975 ft^2 30) 95 ft, 400 ft^2

31) 72 cm, 225 cm^2 32) 120 in, 700 in^2 33) 160 m, 1350 m^2

34) 200 m, 2000 m^2 35) 110 in, 600 in^2 36) 160 m, 1400 m^2

37) 300 in, 4500 in^2 38) 160 ft, 1250 ft^2 39) 96 cm, 450 cm^2

Page 109 (cont.)

40) 166 in, 1440 in^2

Page 110

1) 37.68 in, 113.04 in^2

2) 18.84 in, 28.26 in^2

3) 62.8 cm, 314 cm^2

4) 25.12 cm, 50.24 cm^2

5) 31.4 cm, 78.5 cm^2

6) 43.96 in, 153.86 in^2

7) 314 m, 7850 m^2

8) 188.4 m, 2826 m^2

9) 94.2 m, 706.5 m^2

10) 251.2 cm^2, 5024 m^2

11) 56.52 cm, 254.34 in^2

12) 75.36 cm, 452.16 cm^2

13) 6280 miles, 3,140,000 miles^2

14) 942 ft, 70650ft^2

15) 15,700 m, 19,625,000 m^2

16) 3,140 miles, 785,000 miles^2

17) 1,256 ft, 125,600 ft^2

18) 1,884 cm, .2826 cm^2

19) .785 in, .0490625 in^2

20) 2.826 m, .63585 m^2

21) 44 in, 154 in^2

22) 88 in, 616 in^2

23) 132 cm, 1386 cm^2

24) 220 m, 3850 m^2

25) 440 m, 15,400 m^2

26) 22 ft, 38.5 ft^2

27) 264 ft, 5,544 ft^2

28) 2.2 m, .385 m^2

29) 110 m, 962} m^2

30) 4,400 cm, 1,540,000 cm^2

31) 880 in, 61,600 in^2

32) 352 ft, 9,856 ft^2

33) .88 m, .0616 m^2

34) 572 cm, 26,026 cm^2

35) 33 ft, 86 5/8 ft^2

36) 88 ft, 616 ft^2

37) .44 m, .0154 m^2

38) 16} ft, 21 21/32 ft^2

39) 286 in, 6,506} in^2

40) .22 m, .00385 m^2

Page 111

1) Rectangle, 32 m, 60 m^2

2) Square, 32 in, 64 in^2

3) Right, Scalene Triangle, 30 in, 30 in^2

4) Parallelogram, 60 ft, 180 ft^2

5) Acute, Scalene Triangle, 51 cm, 100 cm^2

6) Trapezoid, 71 cm, 240 cm^2

7) Rectangle
   138 ft, 1,080 ft2

8) Rhombus
   68 in, 221 in^2

9) Acute, Scalene Triangle,
   112 m, 600 m^2

10) Trapezoid,
    98 in, 425 in^2

11) Rhombus,
    100 cm, 500 cm^2

12) Right, Isosceles Triangle,
    87 ft, 312) ft^2

13) Parallelogram,
    120 in, 600 in^2

14) Trapezoid,
    210 in, 2,500 in^2

15) Obtuse, Scalene Triangle,
    100 cm, 440 cm^2

16) Square,
    140 m, 1,225 m^2

17) Trapezoid,
    137 ft, 937.5 ft^2

18) Rectangle,
    30} ft, 57 3/8 ft^2

19) Right, Scalene Triangle,
    48 cm, 96 cm^2

20) Parallelogram
    280 m, 4,000 m^2

21) Square,
    34 cm, 72(cm^2

22) Acute, Scalene Triangle,
    52.6 m, 108 m^2

23) Right, Scalene Triangle,
    168 in, 756 in^2

24) Rectangle,
    95.3 m, 526.35 m^2

25) Trapezoid,
    174.7 ft, 1,515 ft^2

Page 112

1) Rectangle,
   146 ft, 1,260 ft^2

2) Rectangle,
   88 in, 420 in^2

3) Right, Isosceles Triangle,
   68 cm, 200 cm^2

4) Parallelogram,
   64 m, 180 m^2

5) Acute, Scalene Triangle,
   127 ft, 800 ft^2

6) Circle,
   188.4 in, 2,826 in^2

7) Circle,
   94.2 in, 706.5 in^2

8) Circle,
   157 ft, 1,962.5 ft^2

9) Circle,
   220 cm, 3,850 cm^2

10) Circle,
    440 cm, 15,400 cm^2

11) Trapezoid,
    170 m, 1,350 m^2

12) Square,
    20 km, 25 km^2

13) Right, Scalane Triangle,
    120 cm, 600 cm^2

14) Parallelogram,
    110 ft, 630 ft^2

15) Trapezoid,
    150 in, 1,200 in^2

16) Rhombus,
    30 ft, 37.5 ft^2

17) Right, Scalene Traingle,
    180 cm, 1,350 cm^2

18) Rectangle,
    210 cm, 2,700 cm^2

19) Circle,
    66 cm, 346.5 cm^2

20) Trapezoid,
    149 m, 1,235 m^2

21) Acute, Equilateral Triangle,
    225 in, 2,250 in^2

22) Circle,
    7.85 ft, 4.90625 ft^2

23) Parallelogram,
    130 cm, 600 cm^2

24) Rectangle,
    46 1/5 ft, 117 ft^2

25) Circle,
    17.6 m, 24.64 m^2

Page 113

1) Rectangle,
   70 cm, 300 cm^2

2) Right, Scalene Triangle,
   280 ft, 2,100 ft^2

3) Parallelogram,
   32 yd, 45 yd^2

4) Acute, Scalene Triangle,
   88 m, 350 m^2

5) Circle,
   62.8 cm, 314 cm^2

6) Circle,
   314 m, 7,850 m^2

7) Circle,
   88 in, 616 in^2

8) Circle,
   44 ft, 154 ft^2

9) Square,
   120 m, 900 m^2

10) Trapezoid,
    140 in, 1050 in^2

11) Obtuse, Scalene Triangle,
    48 m, 45 m^2

12) Parallelogram,
    130 cm, 800 cm^2

13) Right, Scalene Triangle,
    12 ft, 6 ft^2

14) Trapezoid,
    140 in, 800 in^2

15) Rhombus,
    100 cm, 500 cm^2

16) Rectangle,
    170 ft, 1,500 ft^2

17) Circle,
    157 ft, 1,962.5 ft^2

18) Square,
    29 ft, 52 9/16 ft^2

19) Trapezoid,
    190 m, 1,900 m^2

20) Parallelogram,
    61 m, 155.55 m^2

21) Circle,
    11 in, 9.625 in^2

22) Trapezoid,
    42 ft, 93 ft^2

23) Circle,
    1.884 cm, .2826 cm^2

24) Rectangle,
    61.3 ft, 226.3 ft^2

25) Acute, Scalene Triangle,
    51 47/60 cm, 109 1/2 cm^2

Page 114

1) 512 cm^2, 480 cm^3

2) 340m^2, 400 m^3

3) 900mm^2, 1,800 mm^3

4) 3,150 cm^2, 11,250 cm^3

5) 16,850 mm^2, 146,250 mm^3

6) 2.16 m^2, .216 m^3

7) 25.44 cm^2, 8.64 cm^3

8) .0688 cm^2, .001152 cm^3

9) 13.22 mm^2, 2.856 mm^3

10) 168.944 cm^2, 4,992 cm^3

11) 3 3/8 ft^2, 27/64 ft^3

12) 1 19/30 in^2, 1/8 in^3

13) 23 5/6 yd^2, 7 9/16 yd^3

14) 182 1/15in^2, 164 2/3 in^3

15) 32 5/12 ft^2, 3 1/2 ft^3

16) 72 cm^2, 30 cm^3

17) 270 mm^2, 210mm^3

18) 3.36 m^2, .288 m^3

19) 50.4 cm^2, 13.5 cm^3

20) 1 5/6 in^2, 1/8 in^3

21) 286 cm^2, 280 cm^3

22) 918 m^2, 2,160m^3

23) 2,415 cm^2, 6,750 cm^3

24) 1.88 mm^2, .12 mm^3

25) .2225 m^2, .00525 m^3

26) 816 mm^2, 960 m^3

27) 1 65/144 m^2, 5/96 m^3

28) 60 3/4 ft^2, 18 1/3 ft^3

29) 106 23/48 yd^2, 51 9/16 yd^3

30) 3,465 in^2, 8,100 in^3

Page 115

1) 176 cm^2, 128 cm^3

2) 68 ft^2, 24 ft^3

3) 790 m^2, 1,200 m^3

4) 9,375 mm^2, 50,000 mm^3

5) 170.55 m^2, 119.07 m^3

6) .0528 cm^2, .00054 cm^3

7) 37 3/4 in^2, 10 5/8 in^3

8) 30 3/8 yd.^{2}, 7 yd^3

9) 10 m^2, 1.7 m^3

10) 3,375 in^2, 10,800 in^3

11) 105 cm^2, 40 cm^3

12) 246.5 cm^2, 176 cm^3

13) 1,695 ft^2, 2,275 ft^3

14) 186 m^2, 90 m^3

15) 1.4 m2, .042 m3

16) 11.52 cm2, 1.008 cm3

17) 23 11/12 in2, 4 11/16 in3

18) 82 1/4 ft2, 27 11/32 ft3

19) 31.92 m2, 3.84 m3

20) 33 ft2, 5 1/4 ft3

21) 301.44 cm2, 301.44 cm3

22) 2,355 in2, 7,065 in3

23) 241.152 m2, 45.216 m3

24) 90 3/4 in2, 38 1/2 in3

25) 65.94 cm2, 18.84 cm3

26) 704 m2, 1,078 m3

27) 816.4 ft2, 1,256 ft3

28) 78.4686 cm2, 27.2238 cm3

29) 48 9/28 ft2, 12 4/7 ft3

30) 204.885 ft2, 137.7675 ft3

Page 116

1) 471 cm2, 785 cm3

2) 640.56 cm2, 1,243.44 cm3

3) 659.4 m2, 157 m3

4) 6,280 mm2, 37,680 mm3

5) 7.536 m2, 1.40672 m3

6) 401.92 mm2, 602.88 mm3

7) 85.408 cm2, 60.288 cm3

8) .4396 m2, .01884 m3

9) 2,237.25 mm2, 7,850 mm3

10) 197.82 m2, 211.95 m3

11) 69 1/7 in2, 31 3/7 in3

12) 1,188 ft2, 3,080 ft3

13) 1,106 2/7 in2, 2,816 in3

14) 165 yd2, 154 yd3

15) 4 58/77 in2, 45/77 in3

16) 1,948 4/7 in2, 6,600 in3

17) 3 60/77 ft2, 1/2 ft3

18) 65 9/20 yd2, 40 17/40 yd3

19) 5,885 in2, 34,650 in3

20) 52 5/9 ft2, 25 2/3 ft3

21) 314 cm2, 523 1/3 cm3

22) 1,256 cm2, 4,186 2/3 cm3

23) 1,017.36 cm2, 3,052.08 cm3

24) 1.1304 cm2, .11304 cm3

25) 18.0864 cm2, 7.23456 cm3

26) 452.16 m2, 904.32 m3

27) 10.1736 m2, 3.05208 m3

28) 4.5216 m2, .90432 m3

29) 70,650 cm2, 1,766,250 cm3

30) 2,826 m2, 14,130 m3

31) 616 in2, 1,437 1/3 in3

32) 3 1/7 yd2, 11/21 yd3

33) 113 1/7 ft2, 113 1/7 ft3

34) 154 ft2, 179 2/3 ft3

35) 5,544 in2, 38,808 in3

36) 1,386 yd2, 4,851 yd3

Page 116 (cont.)

37) $5 \ 1/11 \ in^2$, $1 \ 29/363 \ in^3$

38) $38 \ 1/2 \ ft^2$, $22 \ 17/24 \ ft^3$

39) $18/77 \ in^2$, $9/847 in^3$

40) $346 \ 1/2 \ ft^2$, $606 \ 3/8 \ ft^3$

Page 117

1) $484 \ cm^2$, $720 \ cm^3$

2) $294 \ m^2$, $270 \ m^3$

3) $340 \ mm^2$, $300 m^3$

4) $144 \ cm^2$, $72 \ cm^3$

5) $904.32 \ cm^2$, $2,009.6 \ cm^3$

6) $282.6 \ mm^2$, $314 \ mm^3$

7) $5,544 \ m^2$, $38,808 \ m^3$

8) $5.16 \ m^2$, $.72 \ m^3$

9) $10.44 \ cm^2$, $1.62 \ cm^3$

10) $4.56 \ cm^2$, $.432 \ cm^3$

11) $106.92 \ m^2$, $46.98 \ m^3$

12) $.314 \ m^2$, $.01256 \ m^3$

13) $24.64 \ mm^2$, $7.392 \ mm^3$

14) $40.6944 \ cm^2$, $24.41664 \ cm^3$

15) $245 \ 7/25 \ in^2$, $220 \ 1/2 \ in^3$

16) $60 \ 1/7 \ in^2$, $20 \ 4/7 \ in^3$

17) $152 \ 4/9 \ ft^2$, $106 \ 2/3 \ ft^3$

18) $64 \ 7/8 \ in^2$, $18 \ 3/4 \ in^3$

19) $245 \ 1/4 \ in^2$, $189 \ in^3$

20) $180 \ 4/9 \ in^2$, $117 \ 1/3 \ in^3$

21) $7 \ 1/14 \ ft^2$, $1 \ 43/56 \ ft^3$

Page 118

1)   KER,   RES,   LEN,   LEK

2)   NER,   LER,   LES

3)   KES

4)   a: LEK   b: RES   c: REK

5)   a: LES   b: REN   c: LEN   d: KES

6)   a: 70˜   b: 60˜   c: 90˜   d: 100˜   e: 160˜   f: 120˜

7)   a: 60˜   b: 30˜   c: 150˜   d: 65˜   e: 115˜   f: 90˜

8) RYW,   RYT,   BYM,   MYE

9) TYW,   TYE,   BYE,   BYW

10) RYB, RYE, MYT, MYW

11) a: RYT   b: MYE   c: RYW

12)   a: RYW or   b: BYM or c: RYT or d: WYR or e: WYB or f: TYW or
         MYE   RYT   BYM   MYE   TYE   BYE

13)   a: MYE   b: BYM   c: WYB

14)   a: 35˜   b: 55˜   c: 35˜   d: 90˜   e: 90˜   f: 125˜
      g: 145˜   h: 125˜ i: 145˜

15)   a: 40˜   b: 50˜   c: 40˜   d: 90˜   e: 90˜   f: 130˜
      g: 140˜   h: 130˜ i: 140˜

16) ZAP, TAP, TAB, ZAB 17) RAZ, RAI, MAB, MAT

18) TAR, BAR, MAZ, MAP 19) CIP, PIX, XIB, BIC

20) CIN, PIN, RIX, RIA 21) RIP, RIC, AIN, NIX

22) ZRX, MRN 23) MRZ, NRX 24) AZXI

25) AZX, ZXI, XIA, IAZ 26) ARI, ZRX

27) AZR, XIR

28) a: RXZ b: RIX c: AIX d: CIA

29) a: MAT b: CIN c: RXZ d: RZX

30) a: 60° b: 30° c: 60° d: 90° e: 60° f: 30°
    g: 30° h: 60° i: 60° j: 60° k: 60° l: 120°
    m: 120° n: 30° o: 60° p: 90° q: 90°

1) BAT, TAM, MAP, PAY 2) BAP, TAP, TAY

3) YAM 4) a: TAM b: PAM c: TAB

5) a: TAY b: MAY c: PAB d: TAB

6) a: 30° b: 70° c: 100° d: 90° e: 120° f: 160°

7) a: 35° b: 55° c: 30° d: 90° e: 150° f: 125°

8) RUD, DUC, NUL, LUK 9) RUC, CUN, NUK, KUR

10) KUD, NUD, RUL, CUL 11) a: RUD b: NUL c: DUC

12) a: DUK or b: LUC or c: LUN or d: RUD or e: RUC or f: KUR
       CUL   KUD   RUD   LUN   KUN   NUC

13) a: LUN b: KUL c: RUK

14) a: 30° b: 90° c: 60° d: 30° e: 90° f: 150°
    g: 120° h: 120° i: 150° j: 90°

15) a: 33° b: 90° c: 57° d: 33° e: 90° f: 147°
    g: 123° h: 123° i: 147° j: 90°

16) ZXMI 17) ZXM, ZIM, ZIX, XMI

18) ZXN, NIM 19) ZNI, XNM

20) AXB, AXZ, ZXM, BXM 21) AXR, RXB, ZXN, MXN

22)   RXZ, RXM, AXN, NXB   23) TIZ, ZIM, MIP, TIP

24)   TIC, CIP, ZIN, NIM   25) CIZ, CIM, NIP, NIT

26)   ZNX, MNI   27) ZNI, XNM

28) a: INM   b: ZXN   c: ZIN   29) a: IMX b: XZI c: TIC

30) a: NIM   b: NZI   c: NZX   d: NXM

31) a: CIP   b: TIC   c: TIP

32) a: 25°   b: 90°   c: 25°   d: 65°   e: 90°   f: 25°
     g: 65°   h: 50°   i: 130° j: 130° k: 50°   l: 90°
     m: 65°   n: 25°   o: 65°   p: 25°   q: 90°

Page 122

1) 80° 2) 52° 3) 60° 4) 110° 5) 34° 6) 40° 7) 90° 8) 90°

9) 90° 10) 90° 11) 14° 12) 50° 13) 60° 14) 63° 15) 70° 16) 76°

17) 138° 18) 149° 19) 139° 20) 60° 21) 31° 22) 101° 23) 44° 24) 70°

25) 130° 26) 38° 27) 45° 28) 63° 29) 70° 30) 40° 31) 63° 32) 45°

33) 60° 34) 35° 35) 29° 36) 48° 37) 75° 38) 53° 39) 19° 40) 65°

41) 36° 42) 57° 43) 61° 44) 15° 45) 69° 46) 60° 47) 110° 48) 90°

49) 71° 50) 30°

Page 123

1) 65° 2) 50° 3) 45° 4) 34° 5) 30° 6) 5° 7) 75° 8) 60°

9) 58° 10) 39° 11) 62° 12) 36° 13) 15° 14) 83° 15) 24° 16) 150°

17) 120° 18) 90° 19) 135° 20) 80° 21) 70° 22) 30° 23) 105° 24) 75°

25) 165° 26) 95° 27) 60° 28) 36° 29) 93° 30)153°

31) 90° right, scalene   32) 90° right, scalene

33) 42° obtuse, scalene   34) 90° right, isosceles

35) 50° acute, isosceles   36) 90° right, scalene

37) 60° acute scalene   38) 150° obtuse isosceles

39) 23° obtuse, scalene   40) 39° obtuse scalene

41) 60° acute, equilateral   42) 30° acute, isosceles

43) 112o obtuse, scalene   44) 50o acute, isosceles

45) 90o right, scalene   46) 90o right, scalene

47) 45o right, isosceles   48) 52o obtuse, scalene

49) 25o obtuse, isosceles   50) 43o obtuse isosceles

Page 124

1) 10   2) 17   3) 37   4) 25   5) 41   6) 61   7) 45   8) 37

9) 5   10) 29   11) 15   12) 26   13) 50   14) 34   15) 74   16) 65

17) 82   18) 122   19) 25   20) 39   21) 15   22) 35   23) 9   24) 7

25) 12   26) 36   27) 16   28) 8   29) 60   30) 39   31) 220   32) 21

33) 3   34) 13   35) 48   36) 24   37) 21   38) 15   39) 48   40) 120

41) 125   42) 72   43) 89   44) 117   45) 51   46) 317   47) 145   48) 65

49) 73   50) 72

Page 125

1) 5.8, 5.5, 5   2) 103.2, 105;105   3) 17.9, 18, 18   4) 880, 887.5, 90

5) 55.9, 56.5, None   6) 1204.1, 1213, 1213   7) 37.8, 36, 36   8) 14.5, 14.5, 13

9) 78.1, 78, 65 & 78   10) 75, 62.5, 25   11) 94, 94, 93 & 95   12) 310673.2, 348653, None

13) 54, 60, 60   14) 10.5, 10, 10   15) 4723.1, 4171, None   16) 31.2, 31, 27

17) 377.7, 379, 363 & 385   18) 725, 700, 650   19) 49566.9, 49165, 49165   20) 55.1, 58.5, 42

21) 166.2, 170, 175   22) 65.8, 65, 43 & 86   23) 6.1, 6, 7   24) 2369.8, 2387, 2143 & 2343

25) 55, 55, 60

Page 126

1) 10, 10, 10   2) 33, 30, 30   3) 71.5, 71, 70 & 72   4) 180, 181.5, None

5) 6.5, 6.5, 9   6) 43.5, 43.5, 43   7) 1059.6, 1065, 1100   8) 6.5, 6.7, None

Page 126 (cont.)

9) 1.06,
1.0,
.9

10) 12.73,
13,
14.5

11) .0002763,
.000265,
None

12) .3419,
.3445,
.356

13) .01972,
.02,
.02 & .0225

14) 3.56,
3.5,
4.8

15) 1/2,
1/2,
None

16) 17/40,
2/5,
2/5

17) 6 5/9,
4 1/2,
4 1/2 & 5 1/2

18) 3 13/54,
3 1/3,
3 1/3

19) 4 281/294,
4 2/3,
4 2/3 & 6 1/2

20) 5 3/5,
5 5/6,
None

21) 3 3/10,
3 1/2,
3 1/2 & 3 3/4

22) 4.942,
4.75,
4.2

23) 2.9107,
3,
None

24) .1375,
1/8,
1/8

25) .12496,
23/250,
None

Page 127

1) 5/81

2) 1/27

3) 5/54

4) 5/108

5) 5/54

6) 2/27

7) 1/18

8) 1/18

9) 5/108

10) 1/27

11) 2/27

12) 5/81

13) 4/81

14) 25/324

15) 1/9

16) 1/36

17) 10/729

18) 25/972

19) 1/162

20) 8/729

21) 10/153

22) 2/51

23) 4/51

24) 4/51

25) 1/17

26) 5/51

27) 5/102

28) 2/51

29) 5/102

30) 1/17

31) 2/51

32) 10/153

33) 5/51

34) 1/51

35) 1/136

36) 25/816

37) 1/136

38) 1/204

39) 1/68

40) 5/204

41) 1/204

42) 5/612

43) 1/2040

44) 1/306

45) 1/204

46) 1/204

47) 1/3060

48) 1/1020

49) 1/204

50) 5/816

Page 128

1) 1/18

2) 1/12

3) 1/96

4) 1/144

5) 1/24

6) 1/288

7) 1/36

8) 1/48

9) 1/24	10) 1/24	11) 1/9	12) 1/16
13) 1/36	14) 1/64	15) 1/144	16) 1/576
17) 1/36	18) 1/1536	19) 1/64	20) 1/216
21) 2/23	22) 1/23	23) 1/184	24) 1/138
25) 2/23	26) 1/23	27) 1/46	28) 1/92
29) 4/69	30) 1/46	31) 7/69	32) 5/92
33) 1/46	34) 1/92	35) 1/276	36) 0
37) 5/506	38) 3/1012	39) 5/759	40) 7/253
41) 4/759	42) 5/21,252	43) 1/3542	44) 1/3542
45) 4/1771	46) 2/1771	47) 0	48) 1/5313
49) 5/759	50) 1/10,626		

Page 129

1) 1/36	2) 1/9	3) 1/6	4) 5/36
5) 1/12	6) 1/216	7) 1/36	8) 5/108
9) 25/216	10) 1/8	11) 7/72	12) 5/72
13) 1/72	14) 1/1296	15) 35/1296	16) 1/4
17) 1/13	18) 1/52	19) 1/17	20) 1/221
21) 0	22) 11/850	23) 1/5525	24) 11/4165
25) 1/270,725	26) 8/1275	27) 1/1700	28) 33/16,660
29) 8/187,425	30) 1/4165		

Page 130

1) 1/18	2) 1/12	3) 5/36	4) 1/9
5) 1/36	6) 1/72	7) 5/72	8) 7/72
9) 1/8	10) 25/216	11) 5/108	12) 1/36
13) 1/216	14) 1/1296	15) 5/81	16) 1/4
17) 1/13	18) 1/52	19) 3/13	20) 13/204
21) 4/663	22) 8/51	23) 1/102	24) 2/51
25) 169/10,200	26) 78/20,825	27) 1/2652	28) 1/5,997,600
29) 1/649,740	30) 1/4165		

Page 131

1) 33 2) 21 3) 2 4) 0 5) 9 6) 54 7) 32 8) 14

9) 1 10) 16 11) 0 12) 180 13) 10 14) 25 15) 18 16) 44

17) 88 18) 37 19) 20 20) 141 21) 30 22) 3 23) 13 24) 24

25) 52 26) 24 27) 76 28) 39 29) 8 30) 78 31) 77 32) 33

33) 5 34) 15 35) 160 36) 50 37) 11 38) 5 39) 60 40) 28

41) 330 42) 12 43) 64 44) 3 45) 4 46) 31 47) 8 48) 18

49) 32 50) 420

Page 132

1) 28 2) 37 3) 20 4) 47 5) 54 6) 3 7) 4 8) 87

9) 23 10) 66 11) 98 12) 2 13) 49 14) 114 15) 21 16) 23

17) 0 18) 21 19) 39 20) 67 21) 100 22) 161 23) 52 24) 40

25) 134 26) 14 27) 4 28) 109 29) 106 30) 78 31) 45 32) 629

33) 757 34) 20 35) 231 36) 196 37) 163 38) 59 39) 778 40) 291

41) 573 42) 234 43) 90 44) 100 45) 610 46) 113 47) 996 48) 573

49) 393 50) 2999

Page 133

1) 11/12 2) 1/4 3) 7/10 4) 0

5) 1 11/40 6) 54 7) 2 5/6 8) 1 19/24

9) 5 7/10 10) 20/21 11) 11.28 12) 9.793

13) 13.5 14) 3.04 15) 4.52 16) 9.691

17) 77.8 18) 6.27 19) 3.15 20) 2.45

21) 78 22) 17/45 23) 5/18 24) 3 7/30

25) 10 5/16 26) 55/72 27) 403/1008 28) 15 6/13

29) 2 19/22 30) 5 17/25 31) 21.58 32) 22.1

33) 21.9 34) 126.04 35) 42.02 36) 3

37) 64.76	38) 88.4	39) 0	40) 14.5
41) 16	42) 32 1/4	43) 2.225	44) 1 2/5
45) 4.55	46) 4 1/5	47) 0	48) 40
49) .2	50) 258.9		

Page 134

1) 24	2) −20	3) −101	4) 28
5) 7	6) −31	7) 30	8) 10
9) 21	10) 21	11) 0	12) −16
13) −7	14) 360	15) 2	16) 16
17) −32	18) 7	19) −127	20) −33
21) −91	22) 4	23) 16	24) −36
25) 108	26) 130	27) −34	28) −18
29) −40	30) 6	31) −6	32) 0
33) −99	34) −4	35) −60	36) 8
37) 90	38) −2	39) −43	40) 40
41) 78	42) −36	43) −194	44) 14
45) 40	46) 2	47) 372	48) 14
49) −58	50) −252		

Page 135

1) −33	2) 15 1/2	3) −51	4) 20 3/8
5) 8 1/2	6) −11.2	7) 33	8) −18.7
9) 12	10) 19.7	11) 90 2/5	12) 25
13) −12	14) 497.5	15) 6 3/4	16) 11/12
17) −1.3	18) 3/32	19) −16.37	20) −18 3/4
21) −2	22) 3.2	23) 35 1/2	24) −160
25) −19.67	26) −10.37	27) 12.4	28) 42 7/30
29) 7 2/3	30) −9.5	31) 5 3/8	32) 12 5/8

33) 3.7	34) 4.1	35) -182	36) 112 2/3
37) -25 1/2	38) 2.09	39) 2.7	40) 16
41) 35.6	42) -14 1/3	43) -28.95	44) -4.285
45) -525	46) 24.15	47) 156	48) 4.04
49) 4.32	50)- 8 1/2		

Page 136

1) 5	2) 1	3) -6	4) 143
5) -23	6) 217	7) -928	8) -680
9) -199	10) -11	11) -11	12) -384
13) -438	14) 2,000	15) -81	16) -5,684
17) -2,773	18) 463	19) 197	20) -337
21) -442	22) -8,600	23) -9,439	24) 44,147
25) 874	26) -1,780	27) -7	28) -391
29) -166	30) 63	31) -5.51	32) -.708
33) 3.37	34) -.48	35) -999.36	36) 81 1/4
37) 337/864	38) 37/100	39) 504	40) -64 1/2
41) 25 3/4	42) -52.465	43) -372	44) 180
45) -629	46) -154.19	47) -151	48) -.87
49) 47	50) 266		

Page 137

1) 12	2) 65	3) 30	4) 10	5) 100	6) 30	7) 8	8) 0
9) 1	10) 20	11) 940	12) 6	13) 10	14) 6	15) 640	16) 0
17) 75	18) 20	19) 0	20) 25	21) 132	22) 7	23) 456	24) 15
25) 439	26) 4	27) 38	28) 1	29) 88	30) 90	31) 42	32) 42
33) 361	34) 9	35) 115	36) 624	37) 0	38) 0	39) 18	40) 7,21

Page 138

1) 62.8	2) 125.6	3) 94.2	4) 502.4

5) 88	6) 220	7) 440	8) 1.32
9) 40	10) 50	11) 80	12) 400
13) 35	14) 36	15) 37.7	16) 43 1/6
17) 48	18) 75	19) 156.25	20) 17 1/2
21) 3,375	22) 280	23) 765	24) 1,950
25) $150	26) $3,562.50	27) $1,105	28) $264,000
29) 64	30) 32	31) 88	32) 104
33) 785	34) 2,355	35) 1,232	36) 1.155
37) 6,750	38) 27,000	39) 76	40) 1,181.25

Page 139

1) 562.5	2) 600	3) 750	4) 420
5) 240	6) 314	7) 28.26	8) 154
9) 15,400	10) .385	11) 200	12) 1,400
13) 23.75	14) 97 1/2	15) 399	16) 565.2
17) 78,500	18) 7,536	19) 1,848	20) .04928
21) 17,500	22) 2,000	23) 494.8125	24) 42
25) 1,900	26) 48	27) 20.64	28) 4 37/50
29) −2.04	30) 53 3/4	31) 4,186 2/3	32) 523,333 1/3
33) .11304	34) 1,437 1/3	35) .038808	36) 7
37) 316	38) 0	39) −7/32	40) −.25

Page 140

1) 28	2) 42	3) 26	4) 16	5) 37	6) 113	7) 32	8) 70
9) 7	10) 19	11) 31	12) 96	13) 37	14) 94	15) 34	16) 45
17) 101	18) 89	19) 3	20) 88	21) 1	22) 17	23) 7	24) 55
25) 39	26) 45	27) 42	28) 25	29) 9	30) 43	31) 87	32) 43
33) 34	34) 11	35) 110	36) 77	37) 156	38) 86	39) 0	40) 1,112
41) 459	42) 16	43) 50	44) 150	45) 800	46) 12	47) 11	48) 66

49) 54   50) 169

Page 141

1) 38	2) 56	3) 61	4) 343
5) 71	6) 491	7) 24	8) 66
9) 68	10) 55	11) 121	12) 13
13) 324	14) 4 1/2	15) 11 1/2	16) -34
17) 27	18) 50	19) -23	20) -14
21) 15 1/2	22) 10	23) -3.3	24) 3.63
25) .33	26) .93	27) -2.37	28) -2 11/15
29) -2 1/8	30) 6 1/8	31) -7/8	32) 11.5
33) 4.3	34) 20.3	35) 13.1	36) 12.38
37) -5 7/12	38) -2 13/24	39) -3 5/7	40) -2 1/4
41) -2 19/40	42) -1 5/8	43) -4.975	44) -7
45) 0	46) -5 1/2	47) 10.41	48) -4 3/4
49) 7.2	50) -1 19/24		

Page 142

1) 7	2) 175	3) 12	4) 13
5) 54	6) 30	7) 12	8) 9
9) 80	10) 140	11) 19	12) 14
13) 30	14) 210	15) 17	16) 7
17) 220	18) 320	19) 20	20) 15
21) 960	22) 648	23) 8	24) 108
25) 162	26) 27	27) 18	28) 3
29) 8	30) 9	31) 360	32) 400
33) 140	34) 1,200	35) 1,200	36) 6
37) 4	38) 3	39) 2	40) 16
41) 150	42) 240,000	43) 1,400	44) 45

45) 3,750	46) 13	47) 1,700	48) 1,260
49) 480	50) 5,000		

Page 143

1) 15	2) 960	3) 150	4) −15
5) 15	6) 45	7) −24	8) 24
9) 1.5	10) .025	11) 12	12) 432
13) −14	14) −1,400	15) .14	16) 64
17) −20	18) 2,000	19) −48	20) 6.86
21) .14	22) −6	23) 5	24) −.002
25) −3	26) −90	27) 90	28) .03
29) 3,000	30) −1.5	31) .05	32) 9.8
33) −14	34) −1,400	35) .026	36) 2/15
37) 1 1/9	38) −1 1/3	39) 1 3/5	40) 400
41) −4	42) .0004	43) 1/12	44) −3 2/3
45) −12.5	46) 112.5	47) 1	48) .08
49) −2/5	50) .4		

Page 144

1) 56	2) 9	3) 70	4) 441
5) 15	6) 375	7) 70	8) 80
9) 5	10) 72	11) 48	12) 720
13) 34	14) 300	15) 15	16) 10
17) 67	18) 13	19) 1,170	20) 48
21) 850	22) 3	23) 10,000	24) 79
25) 247	26) 61	27) 10,000	28) 28
29) 53	30) 9	31) 0	32) 20
33) 86	34) 1,183	35) 7	36) 104
37) 8	38) 80	39) 210	40) 407

41) 35	42) 12	43) 162	44) 3
45) 450	46) 539	47) 1,350	48) 40
49) 75,000	50) 302		

Page 145

1) 27	2) 45	3) 4	4) 324
5) 40	6) 35.1	7) 36.9	8) −4
9) 2 1/4	10) 4	11) −35	12) 21
13) 13 1/3	14) 52.7	15) 30	16) −36
17) −3	18) −15	19) 11 1/5	20) 15
21) 8.12	22) −.015	23) 2/3	24) −7/15
25) 48	26) 448	27) 64	28) 7
29) −700	30) −.007	31) −48	32) 55 7/8
33) .685	34) 1.9	35) 4.69	36) 40
37) −6	38) −6 1/3	39) 0	40) −20
41) −7	42) −1/8	43) −1 31/40	44) −1 9/16
45) −33,600	46) −.89	47) 600	48) .76
49) −5	50) 337.1		

Page 146

1) 4	2) 60	3) 36	4) 576
5) −400	6) 47.88	7) 49.2	8) −.004
9) −64	10) 47 1/4	11) 34	12) −.3
13) 11.9	14) −300	15) −867	16) 3 11/12
17) −3 1/3	18) −.15	19) −2 1/12	20) −128/375
21) −29/48	22) −1 2/5	23) 400	24) 45
25) 59.85	26) 9	27) −3.7	28) 56.3
29) 10.26	30) −10.26	31) −2	32) 3
33) −.04	34) 5.76	35) −37	36) 2,000

37) 14   38) 117   39) 1,134   40) .06

41) −4.7   42) −7.88   43) 800   44) .008

45) −81   46) 53 1/3   47) 1/5   48) 8.8

49) −24.875   50) .005

Page 147

1) 2   2) 3   3) 5   4) 7   5) 14   6) 7   7) 7   8) 8

9) 13   10) 9   11) 0   12) 6   13) 9   14) 26   15) 13   16) 12

17) 13   18) 61   19) 18   20) 7   21) 4   22) 7   23) 7   24) 13

25) 19   26) 11   27) 14   28) 3   29) 8   30) 3   31) 5   32) 9

33) 2   34) 12   35) 16   36) 18   37) 20   38) 18   39) 18   40) 3

41) 6   42) 6   43) 17   44) 4   45) 24   46) 4   47) 4   48) 15

49) 124   50) 48

Page 148

1) 13   2) 15   3) 17   4) 16

5) 21   6) 4   7) 24   8) 149

9) 24   10) 8   11) −9   12) −10

13) −8   14) 10   15) −12   16) 6

17) −50   18) −9   19) −23   20) 7

21) 60   22) −8   23) 62   24) .02

25) −100   26) 192   27) 40   28) 900

29) −1 1/4   30) 2 22/45   31) 2/3   32) −3

33) .004   34) −2 5/8   35) −5.5   36) −550

37) −4/5   38) −200   39) 5   40) 27,600

41) 1 1/4   42) 25   43) −10 1/2   44) 5

45) 3   46) −12   47) −.4   48) 1/20

49) .015   50) 80.05

Page 149

1) 70 2) 6 3) 98 4) 1176 5) 54 6) 6 7) 21 8) 15

9) 65 10) 6 11) 1014 12) 91 13) 9 14) 16 15) 11 16) 52

17) 16 18) 2 19) 20 20) 41 21) 15 22) 23 23) 40 24) 13

25) 5 26) 8 27) 37 28) 36 29) 7 30) 4 31) 23 32) 186

33) 37 34) 9 35) 26 36) 28 37) 174 38) 16 39) 21 40) 80

41) 106 42) 954 43) 315 44) 8 45) 2 46) 23 47) 6 48) 39

49) 1764 50) 206

Page 150

1) 88 2) 12 3) 768 4) 95.2

5) −12 6) −1,200 7) 104 8) 95.92

9) −7.04 10) −.12 11) 9 12) 9

13) 11 14) 11 15) 0 16) −144

17) −240 18) .06 19) 4 20) −1,080

21) 15.23 22) 19 23) 14 24) −3 1/3

25) −48 26) .064 27) −1/10 28) −4.2

29) 5 30) 48 31) 4 32) −500

33) 59.88 34) 110 35) −78,000 36) 24

37) −315 38) 3 39) 23.16 40) 24.51

41) 1 7/8 42) 1 7/25 43) 1 17/40 44) 13

45) −1 46) 6 47) 39 48) −21

49) −2014 50) −20.03

Page 151

1) 3 2) 7 3) 3 4) 8 5) 6 6) 17 7) 32 8) 7

9) 8 10) 9 11) 7 12) 4 13) 6 14) 15 15) 7 16) 5

17) 8 18) 4 19) 12 20) 140 21) 3 22) 19 23) 3 24) 19

25) 6 26) 6 27) 6 28) 14 29) 2 30) 4 31) 13 32) 13

33) 17 34) 12 35) 20 36) 4 37) 26 38) 13 39) 19 40) 12

41) 6   42) 5   43) 12   44) 4   45) 12   46) 20   47) 23   48) 6

49) 4   50) 3

Page 152

1) 2	2) 7	3) 9	4) 6
5) −9	6) −12	7) 1 1/2	8) 2 1/2
9) .04	10) .08	11) 4	12) −16
13) −36	14) 190	15) .03	16) 30
17) −30	18) −3 1/2	19) .002	20) −.0806
21) −16	22) 5	23) −4	24) −18 1/2
25) −5	26) −18 1/2	27) 5	28) −.08
29) −.02	30) −.04	31) −.06	32) .08
33) 40	34) −80	35) −7 4/5	36) 6
37) 26	38) 6	39) 26	40) .28
41) .08	42) −12	43) −21	44) −39
45) .014	46) 24	47) −20	48) −3
49) −3	50) 50		

Page 153

1) 4	2) 16	3) 24	4) 7	5) 13	6) 9	7) 7	8) 49
9) 33	10) 7	11) 8	12) 21	13) 3	14) 2	15) 4	16) 13
17) 7	18) 5	19) 23	20) 27	21) 19	22) 14	23) 63	24) 7
25) 17	26) 9	27) 8	28) 6	29) 16	30) 4	31) 9	32) 7
33) 16	34) 4	35) 29	36) 2	37) 24	38) 13	39) 6	40) 20
41) 6	42) 20	43) 15	44) 24	45) 14	46) 5	47) 8	48) 60
49) 90	50) 45						

Page 154

1) 13	2) 3	3) 15	4) 12
5) 7.5	6) 6	7) 4	8) 24

9) −24   10) −4   11) 18   12) 12

13) −19   14) 5   15) 12   16) 5

17) 2 1/2   18) −2   19) −23   20) 8

21) 4   22) −.09   23) 40   24) −80

25) .0005   26) −70   27) −60   28) 1 3/5

29) 1 1/5   30) −3 3/4   31) −10   32) −6

33) −144/289   34) .03   35) .03   36) 300

37) 2,000   38) −370   39) −1,875   40) −60

41) 130   42) −40   43) 50   44) 80

45) 30   46) −70   47) −80   48) −600

49) −.005   50) .005

Page 155

1) 78   2) 90   3) 14   4) 504   5) 18   6) 24   7) 7   8) 21

9) 28   10) 12   11) 48   12) 13   13) 9   14) 93   15) 27   16) 5

17) 7   18) 17   19) 11   20) 14   21) 9   22) 3   23) 4   24) 9

25) 5   26) 9   27) 53   28) 18   29) 9   30) 450   31) 10   32) 272

33) 0   34) 12   35) 70   36) 3   37) 36   38) 80   39) 3   40) 5

41) 36   42) 824   43) 24   44) 47   45) 8   46) 100   47) 3   48) 24

49) 30   50) 27

Page 156

1) 91   2) 105   3) 14   4) 686

5) 24   6) 25   7) 16 1/3   8) 49

9) 49   10) −147   11) 97 1/3   12) −17

13) 8   14) 7   15) −108   16) −4

17) −11/24   18) −12   19) −2.97   20) .05

21) 9 7/8   220 −.0075   23) −9,000   24) 1.65

25) .003   26) −9   27) 16 1/2   28) .005

29) -11	30) -9	31) 27 1/2	32) -12,500
33) 45	34) -.35	35) 60	36) -5/6
37) .00307	38) -67.5	39) -2.48	40) 50
41) -50	42) 12	43) 19	44) 2.85
45) -.013	46) -3	47) 30	48) -2
49) .87	50) -.023		

Page 157

1) 21	2) 9	3) 19	4) 21	5) 13	6) 16	7) 1	8) 4
9) 46	10) 3	11) 19	12) 1	13) 37	14) 2	15) 7	16) 12
17) 49	18) 17	19) 8	20) 8	21) 12	22) 11	23) 4	24) 12
25) 4	26) 205	27) 97	28) 24	29) 15	30) 2	31) 3	32) 215
33) 9	34) 8	35) 3	36) 3	37) 19	38) 14	39) 3	40) 45
41) 7	42) 7	43) 6	44) 9	45) 38	46) 14	47) 77	48) 130
49) 19	50) 63						

Page 158

1) 2	2) 3	3) 2	4) 2
5) -3	6) -3	7) -2	8) -7
9) 10	10) -11 1/2	11) -20	12) 200
13) -40	14) .075	15) .021	16) -1/3
17) .02	18) -30	19) 10.2	20) 12
21) -20	22) -30	23) -208	24) -7.05
25) 0	26) .4	27) 3 2/3	28) .13
29) 1 1/2	30) 7 1/2	31) -300	32) 50
33) -352	34) 40	35) 560	36) 12
37) 300	38) -280	39) .002	40) -.04
41) 2/3	42) 5/6	43) -.01	44) -1 1/3
45) -.025	46) -.001	47) -1	48) -2

49) -30   50) .501

1) 96	2) 9	3) 120	4) 1296	5) 6	6) 12	7) 6	8) 18
9) 12	10) 15	11) 31	12) 13	13) 208	14) 11	15) 12	16) 17
17) 16	18) 719	19) 5	20) 21	21) 486	22) 112	23) 14	24) 133
25) 9	26) 16	27) 12	28) 48	29) 96	30) 22	31) 16	32) 134
33) 23	34) 188	35) 15	36) 72	37) 289	38) 14	39) 24	40) 60
41) 12	42) 14	43) 38	44) 14	45) 34	46) 50	47) 9	48) 40
49) 5	50) 3						

1) -4	2) 14	3) 16 1/4	4) -24
5) -8	6) -72	7) 1 2/3	8) -.09
9) 6.14	10) -39 1/2	11) -300	12) 4.5
13) -5	14) 7	15) -13	16) -11.05
17) 5.18	18) 150	19) .204	20) .013
21) -.024	22) 1.2	23) -4.31	24) -300
25) .0015	26) 12	27) 8	28) -4.8
29) -2/3	30) -1 1/5	31) -1 3/8	32) -138
33) -2/3	34) 5/6	35) 200	36) .6
37) -.03	38) -68,000	39) 3.9995	40) -34
41) .005	42) .03	43) 1.306	44) -.071
45) -1	46) -3	47) 1 1/3	48) -.0075
49) .375	50) -200		

1) 6	2) 13	3) 5	4) 1 1/3
5) 2	6) -5	7) -4	8) -14
9) -5	10) -10	11) -13	12) 13

13) 27	14) -27	15) -4	16) -8
17) -32 1/2	18) 15	19) 6 1/2	20) 4
21) 1/3	22) 1/5	23) -1 1/2	24) -2 31/36
25) -21.5	26) 17	27) -1 1/2	28) -16 1/2
29) -12.5	30) 69	31) .6	32) .6
33) -152 1/2	34) -85 1/3	35) .075	36) 6
37) 3/4	38) -8 1/2	39) -1	40) 5/24
41) -48	42) .25	43) -3/8	44) 8.25
45) -12.2	46) 29	47) -3	48) 3
49) -.9	50) 30.2		

Page 162

1) 25	2) -5	3) 7	4) 7
5) -9 3/5	6) -1/8	7) -1	8) -26 1/2
9) 11	10) 7	11) 7	12) -7
13) 5	14) -1.56	15) -.4	16) -1.12
17) 6	18) -36	19) 4	20) -.0075
21) -.075	22) .13	23) -5	24) -.9
25) 2.6	26) 0	27) 59	28) 7
29) -.602	30) 12	31) -7/8	32) 15
33) 1.825	34) -.084	35) 3	36) -.006
37) -120,000	38) 1/6	39) .0025	40) .0424
41) 3 3/4	42) 15	43) -7 1/2	44) 1 2/3
45) -540	46) .75	47) 48	48) 2 1/4
49) 26	50) -4.005		

Page 163

1) M > 32	2) M < 48	3) M > 5	4) M < 320
5) M $\geq$ 32	6) M $\leq$ 48	7) M $\geq$ 5	8) M $\leq$ 320

9) $M \geq 14$ 10) $M > 14$ 11) $P \leq 8$ 12) $I \leq 63$

13) $T \geq 62$ 14) $T < 205$ 15) $S > 0$ 16) $B \geq 0$

17) $V > 7$ 18) $R \leq 7$ 19) $G > 1183$ 20) $H \leq 78$

21) $P \geq 104$ 22) $A > 33$ 23) $N \leq 3$ 24) $T \geq 10$

25) $H < 56$ 26) $E \geq 7$ 27) $R > 7$ 28) $S < 48$

29) $M > 4$ 30) $M \geq 4$ 31) $M < 2$ 32) $N \leq 88$

33) $N > 88$ 34) $N \geq 12$ 35) $N \leq 18$ 36) $N \geq 16$

37) $N \geq 9$ 38) $N < 6$ 39) $N \leq 4$ 40) $N < 3$

41) $M \geq 33$ 42) $M > 39$ 43) $M \leq 23$ 44) $M \leq 5$

45) $M < 5$ 46) $M < 54$ 47) $M < 36$ 48) $M > 3$

49) $M \geq 250$ 50) $M < 250{,}000$

Page 164

1) $N > -3$ 2) $N \geq 13$ 3) $N \leq -13$ 4) $N \leq 3$

5) $N \geq 6$ 6) $N > -6$ 7) $N < -6$ 8) $N \leq 6$

9) $N < 0$ 10) $N \leq -3$ 11) $M \geq 7$ 12) $M \leq -7$

13) $M < 6$ 14) $M < -6$ 15) $M > -6$ 16) $M > 6$

17) $N > 15$ 18) $N \geq -9$ 19) $N \leq -21$ 20) $N \leq 13$

21) $N \geq -8$ 22) $N \leq 8$ 23) $N \geq -6\ 3/4$ 24) $N \geq -5\ 1/4$

25) $N < 17/24$ 26) $M < 2.3$ 27) $I < -4$ 28) $S < 2.93$

29) $S \geq 18.63$ 30) $I > .5$ 31) $S \geq 50$ 32) $S \leq -50$

33) $I \leq -.05$ 34) $P < -19{,}000$ 35) $P > 2.397$ 36) $I \geq -24.29$

37) $R \geq 14/15$ 38) $E < 2\ 9/20$ 39) $B \leq -22/25$ 40) $E \geq 25/36$

41) $L \geq -1/2$ 42) $S \geq -4/5$ 43) $X \leq 2$ 44) $Z > -410$

45) $L < 1.225$ 46) $M > 6.73$ 47) $R \leq .3$ 48) $T > 5$

49) $B \geq -3\ 1/3$ 50) $B > -4\ 5/7$

Page 165

1) $M > 6$ 2) $M < 4$ 3) $M \geq 9$ 4) $M \leq 5$

5) M > 2	6) M < 2	7) M ≥ 0	8) M ≥ 2
9) M ≤ 2	10) M < 2	11) S < 1	12) M > 3
13) U > 5	14) M < 47	15) U ≤ 7	16) S ≥ 3
17) T ≥ 25	18) A ≤ 1	19) N > 3	20) G < 2
21) S ≥ 15	22) N ≥ 0	23) N < 6	24) N < 2
25) N ≥ 8	26) N ≤ 4	27) N > 16	28) N < 48
29) N ≤ 9	30) N ≥ 36	31) N > 3	32) N ≥ 24
33) N ≤ 72	34) N < 17	35) N ≤ 4	36) M > 4
37) M > 3	38) T < 4	39) R < 9	40) B ≥ 5
41) B ≥ 5	42) C ≤ 6	43) C ≤ 3	44) R > 3
45) R > 2	46) A < 4	47) A < 5	48) B ≥ 8
49) B ≥ 13	50) T ≤ 351		

1) N > -2	2) N ≥ -2	3) N ≤ 4	4) N < -2
5) N ≥ 3	6) N < -9	7) N ≤ -9	8) N ≥ -23
9) N < 7	10) N > 17	11) M ≥ -18	12) M ≤ 21
13) M ≥ -21	14) M > -6	15) M ≥ -30	16) M < 30
17) M > -20	18) M ≤ -1	19) M ≤ -13	20) M ≤ .72
21) M < -.8	22) R ≥ -.02	23) R > 2,000	24) R ≥ -20
25) R ≤ .015	26) R ≥ 1 1/2	27) R < 36	28) R ≥ 15.5
29) R ≤ .01	30) R > 120	31) R < 120	32) T < 8
33) T < .02	34) T ≥ -2.0075	35) T ≤ 15	36) T ≤ 60
37) T < 60	38) T > 0	39) T ≥ 0	40) T < 6,000
41) B ≥ -.025	42) B ≥ -6.15	43) B ≤ -.9	44) B < -.35
45) A > 12	46) A ≥ 10	47) A < 4	48) A ≤ 5
49) A < 7.5	50) A ≤ -100		

1) N > 9	2) N < 4	3) N ≥ -4	4) N ≥ 15
5) N > 2	6) N < -2	7) N ≤ 4.8	8) N ≥ -4 4/5
9) N ≥ 4	10) N > - 2 1/2	11) N > 2 1/2	12) L > -4
13) S < 2	14) U ≥ -13	15) T < 0	16) I > 8
17) G ≥ 16	18) E < -1/4	19) R ≤ -13	20) S ≥ 0
21) M > 6 1/3	22) M < - 6 1/3	23) N < 5.2	24) N ≥ -5
25) N ≥ -2.4	26) N ≤ 5	27) N ≥ -1.6	28) N < -1/4
29) N ≤ -4	30) N ≥ 2.03	31) N ≤ -.006	32) N ≤ -600
33) N ≤ -2.995	34) R > 2 2/9	35) R ≤ -52	36) T ≥ 11/15
37) T < 38 1/4	38) B ≤ 17.75	39) B ≤ .71	40) A ≥ -2/3
41) A ≤ 1 1/3	42) Z ≥ 20	43) Z < -2 7/9	44) T > -1 1/5
45) L < -.0003	46) .005	47) Y ≤ -319	48) Y ≥ 23,000
49) T ≥ -.015	50) T < 0		

1) N > 3	2) N > 12	3) N < 13	4) N < 2
5) N ≥ 3	6) N ≤ 6	7) N < 4	8) N > 5
9) N ≤ 5	10) N ≥ 3	11) M > 7	12) M ≤ 7
13) M ≥ 3	14) M < 14	15) M < 6	16) M < 43
17) M > 26	18) M ≥ 71	19) M < 15	20) M ≤ 16
21) R > 7	22) R < 11	23) R ≥ 13	24) R ≤ 17
25) R > 7	26) R < 46	27) R ≤ 16	28) R ≥ 19
29) R > 14	30) R < 2	31) T ≥ 12	32) M ≥ 4
33) M < 14	34) B < 7	35) A ≤ 13	36) T > 27
37) Z ≤ 7	38) Z > 4	39) Z ≥ 74	40) L > 13
41) N ≥ 20	42) M < 19	43) R > 5	44) T ≥ 4
45) W < 3	46) Y > 26	47) R < 48	48) R ≤ 6
49) Z ≥ 37	50) R ≤ 17		

1) L > 13	2) L ≥ 17	3) A ≤ 9	4) A ≥ 13
5) T > -6	6) T < -15	7) H ≤ -8	8) H < 19
9) C > -12	10) C ≤ -14	11) A > -22	12) A ≥ -17
13) R ≥ -13	14) R < -23	15) T ≥ -14	16) T < 36
17) E ≤ 6	18) E < 20	19) R ≥ 10	20) R ≤ -30
21) W > -1/4	22) U > -2	23) E ≥ -.9	24) E > 5
25) C ≥ 2	26) C ≥ .17	27) A ≥ 130	28) A > -2.5
29) N > -40	30) N ≥ -800	31) H < -.28	32) H < -28
33) A ≥ -310	34) A < -90	35) N ≥ -8	36) N ≤ -12
37) P < -30	38) D ≤ 20	39) L ≤ 1	40) L < -5
41) E ≥ 72	42) E ≥ -4	43) E > 195	44) I ≤ -240
45) T > -13	46) T ≥ -.3	47) W > -.3	48) W > -16
49) W ≥ -2.7	50) W < 18.4		

1) N ≥ -3.4	2) N ≤ .2	3) N > 5	4) N ≤ 6
5) N < .04	6) N ≤ 1.7	7) N > .7	8) N ≥ -.2
9) N < -8	10) N ≥ .7	11) N ≥ -2.15	12) N ≤ -2
13) N ≥ 1.9	14) N > .7	15) N ≥ .07	16) N ≥ 1 2/3
17) N < -1.7	18) N < -.8	19) N > -1	20) N ≤ -.625
21) P ≤ .06	22) I > 20	23) T < 35	24) T ≥ 4.03
25) S < .6	26) B ≥ -270	27) V < -1/5	28) R < 4
29) G ≥ .02	30) H > 500	31) P > 14.97	32) A > -.029
33) N ≥ -2.3	34) T > -.7	35) H ≥ .075	36) E > .08
37) R < -1.73	38) S ≥ 25	39) M ≤ -1/9	40) M > .02
41) M > 4	42) N ≤ -5	43) R ≥ 11	44) R ≥ -.0125
45) R > -2	46) R ≤ 21	47) M < 3	48) M ≥ -1/4
49) N ≤ 1	50) N > 3		

1) $N + 7 = 21$; 14

2) $N - 7 = 21$; 28

3) $7N = 21$; 3

4) $N / 7 = 21$; 147

5) $N + 24 = 43$; 19

6) $N - 39 = 21$; 60

7) $5N = 55$; 11

8) $8N = 96$; 12

9) $2N + 5 = 43$; 19

10) $3N - 7 = 29$; 12

11) $8N + 1 = 65$; 8

12) $9N - 13 = 95$; 12

13) $7N + 8 = 99$; 13

14) $6N + 3N = 117$; 13

15) $5N - 2N = 42$; 14

16) $7N + 8N = 45$; 3

17) $6N + n = 84$; 12

18) $4N - N = 87$; 29

19) $8N = 6N + 34$; 17

20) $9N = 5N + 56$; 14

21) $4N = 2N + 104$; 52

22) $3N = N + 78$; 39

23) $17N = 4N + 182$; 14

24) $6N + 1 = 2N + 21$; 5

25) $7N + 17 = 3N + 109$; 23

26) $15N - 8 = 3N + 76$; 7

27) $12N - 34 = 5N + 36$; 10

28) $21N + 17 = 10N + 160$; 13

29) $14N - 33 = 5N + 12$; 5

30) $5N + 31 = 151$; 24

31) $5N + 3N - 2N = 54$; 9

32) $14N = 11N + 57$; 19

33) $12N - 28 = 5N$; 4

34) $18N + 1 = N + 52$; 3

35) $16N = 12N - 9N + 52$; 4

1) $N + 24 = 31$; 7

2) $N + 18 = 13$; −5

3) $N - 5 = 27$; 32

4) $N - 31 = -54$; −23

5) $N + 29 = -18$; −47

6) $N - 15 = -24$; −9

7) $4N = 56$; 14

8) $2N = 17$; 8 1/2

9) $1/3N = 14$; 42

10) $.5N = -75$; −150

11) $3/4N = 12$; 16

12) $N + 1/2 = 24$; 23 1/2

13) $N - 2/3 = -17$; −16 1/3

14) $N + 8 = 0$; −8

15) $3N - 5 = -32$; −9

16) $3 + 4N = 31$; 7

17) −7N − 6 = 85; −13

18) 2N + 140 = 14; −63

19) 3/5N + 12 = −15; −45

20) 5N + 4N = 72; 8

21) 8N + N = .513; .057

22) 6N − N = 85; 17

23) −5N + −7N = 84; −7

24) 4N − 7N = 48; −16

25) 3/4N + 2/3N = 51; 36

26) 8N = N + 147; 21

27) 5N = 2N + 42; 14

28) 6N = 8N + 66; −33

29) 4N = 7N − 42; 14

30) 3N + 7 = N + 29; 11

31) 9N − 5= 90 + 4N; 19

32) 8N + 13 = −92 + 3N; −21

33) 8N − 13 = 97 − 3N; 10

34) 57 + 12N = 9N; −19

35) 14N + 4 − 5N = N − 16; −2 1/2

Pages 175 – 176

1) N + 9 = 54; 45

2) N − 9 = 54; 63

3) 9N = 56; 6

4) N / 9 = 54; 486

5) −9N = 54; −6

6) 2/3N = 54; 81

7) N + 2/3 = 54; 53 1/3

8) 4N − 5 = 47; 13

9) 2N + 8 = 82; 37

10) −5N + 1 = 86; −17

11) 1/2N − 7 = −18; −22

12) .16N + 44 = 12; −200

13) 4N + 3N = 42; 6

14) 8N − 3N = −75; −15

15) 8N + 9N = −51; −3

16) 20N − N = 95; 5

17) 3/5N + 5/6N = −86; −60

18) 14N = 3n + 132; 12

19) 5N = 9N + 28; −7

20) 15N = N − 42; −3

21) 15N = 48 − N; 3

22) 3/5N = 1/2N − 25; −250

23) 8N −1 = 2N + 41; 7

24) 7N + 3 = N + 87; 14

25) 4N − 21 = 54 + 7N; −25

26) 7 + 13N = −5N + 61; 3

27) 8N + 7 = 52 + 1/2N; 6

28) 4N + 1 = 85; 21

29) 4N + N = 85; 17

30) 10N = −3N + 91; 7

31) 14N = 5N + 91 + 2N; 13

32) 25N + 7 = 59 − N; 2

33) $-17N = 18N + .14; -.004$ 34) $9N + 10N - 14N = 3.1; .62$

35) $2N = 1.7N + 153; 510$

Pages 177 - 178

1) $N + 15 = 45; 30$ 2) $N - 15 = 45;; 60$

3) $15N = 45; 3$ 4) $1/15N = 45; 675$

5) $N + 45 = 15; -30$ 6) $-8N = 32; -4$

7) $N + 1/2 = 7; 6 1/2$ 8) $2N = -24; -12$

9) $5N - 3 = 42; 9$ 10) $6N + 1 = 43; 7$

11) $-3N + 5 = 56; -17$ 12) $7N + 24 = -67; -13$

13) $3N - 1/2 = 17.5; 6$ 14) $8N - 4N = 48; 12$

15) $8N + 4N = 48; 4$ 16) $-8N + 4N = 48; -12$

17) $.7N + 1.5N = 176; 80$ 18) $1/2N - 3/4N = 13; -52$

19) $4N = 8N + 76; -19$ 20) $6N = 7N + 41; -41$

21) $5N = 2N - 42; -14$ 22) $5N = 42 - 2N; 6$

23) $1.8N = 3/5N + 156; 130$ 24) $9N + 3 = 8N -6; -9$

25) $12N + 1 = 4N -3; -1/2$ 26) $7N - 7 = -5N +89; 8$

27) $3/4N + 15 = 1/6N - 69; -144$ 28) $3.5N + 8 = 3n + -28; -72$

29) $3N + 8N = 7N - .56; -.14$ 30) $5N = 3N + 4N + 8; -4$

31) $6N + 1 = 48; 8$ 32) $6N + N = 49; 7$

33) $-7N + -5N = -15N + .18; .06$ 34) $N = 2/7N + 15; 21$

35) $9.36N = 9N - 144; -400$

* * * * * **PRACTICE** ***** **PRACTICE** ***** **PRACTICE** * * * * *

B O O K   I   C O V E R S

Whole Numbers	#	Prime Numbers
Decimals	$	G C F
Rounding	%	L C M
Money	+	Fractions
Place Value	−	

If you need more information, contact:
ST2 Publishing, 203 Si Town Road, Castle Rock, WA 98611
(206) 274-7242

1) 3,711	2) 674	3) 2,957	4) 103
5) 31,088	6) 6,142	7) 24,038	8) 307,945
9) 18,094	10) 814	11) 2,003	12) 752
13) 5.56	14) 922.2	15) 25.318	16) $55.90
17) 3.784	18) 20.21	19) 2.052	20) 29.71
21) $14.29	22) 144.42	23) .1071	24) $5.05
25) $3.35	26) .0075	27) 34,600	28) 11.6
29) 875	30) $301.38	31) 6 3/20	32) 54 2/15
33) 480 5/8	34) 4 2/5	35) 4 35/36	36) 20 11/36
37) 50 35/48	38) 758 53/72	39) 5	40) 3/16
41) 1 2/3	42) 3/25	43) 15	44) 2
45) 128/675	46) 5 1/3	47) 4/15	48) 4.675 or 4 27/40
49) $240.36	50) 20.705		

1) 1,510	2) 1,576	3) 8,253	4) 369
5) 1,009	6) 2,028	7) 7,200	8) 17,646
9) 566,212	10) 1,502	11) 2,003	12) 504
13) 9.17	14) 90.76	15) 461.08	16) 86.7
17) 93.9	18) 40.04	19) 441.318	20) $16.42
21) 27.68	22) 3.1044	23) .000408	24) $7.15
25) .00903	26) 375	27) 28	28) $2.01
29) 4 7/24	30) 50 27/28	31) 2 1/6	32) 44 77/90
33) 3/20	34) 3 9/40	35) 22 17/18	36) 402 2/5
37) 1/4	38) 20	39) 2	40) 5/8
41) 1 1/7	42) 2/3	43) 1	44) 1/2
45) 1.725	46) 29/30	47) 6.43	48) $240.49
49) $28.60	50) 64.78		

Page 181

1) 1,583	2) 1,798	3) 6,139	4) 8,569
5) 5,419	6) 46,151	7) 5,358	8) 28,618
9) 682,816	10) 1,386	11) .27	12) 3,952
13) 18.92	14) 6.45	15) 7.354	16) $18.59
17) 68.54	18) 36.02	19) 61.29	20) $5.42
21) 68.284	22) .34595	23) .8064	24) $580.02
25) .0504	26) 20.05	27) 21,300	28) $3.60
29) 67/84	30) 1 28/45	31) 12 19/45	32) 48 2/3
33) 13/40	34) 41/80	35) 8 19/42	36) 8 43/54
37) 30/49	38) 7/16	39) 22 2/5	40) 131 67/100
41) 1 9/40	42) 9/13	43) 1 23/31	44) 4/9
45) 52.5	46) .95	47) 13.65	48) 70.4
49) 12.58	50) 2.52		

Page 182

1) 1,031	2) 1,684	3) 7,412	4) 7,479
5) 7,559	6) 88,528	7) 4,012	8) 41,078
9) 287,584	10) 935 R4	11) 3,463 R9	12) 1,246 R5
13) 14.99	14) 5.01	15) 2.436	16) $24.52
17) 84.93	18) 58.23	19) 30.58	20) $13.64
21) 48.894	22) .43776	23) .4611	24) $209.41
25) .0087	26) 1.888	27) 156,000	28) $9.35
29) 1 11/24	30) 1 29/60	31) 13 11/60	32) 38 71/72
33) 29/100	34) 39/112	35) 2 103/120	36) 11 17/27
37) 18/35	38) 3/13	39) 36	40) 46 2/3
41) 2 21/22	42) 1	43) 1 1/2	44) 14 14/15
45) 36	46) 3.84375	47) 44.6	48) 8
49) 9.22	50) 4 3/5		

Page 183

1) 1,074	2) 9,367	3) 93,217	4) 239
5) 6,169	6) 24,995	7) 3,120	8) 66,597
9) 380,538	10) 140 R6	11) 131 R35	12) 190 R38
13) 7.275	14) 37.364	15) 23.6843	16) $27.43
17) 5.76	18) 8.8035	19) 7.14	20) $4.64
21) .0576	22) 4.128	23) .008436	24) $26.60
25) .17775	26) 19.68	27) 30.4	28) $.54
29) 1 7/15	30) 1 11/24	31) 13 11/60	32) 26 11/36
33) 4/45	34) 11/24	35) 1 4/21	36) 2 11/30
37) 3/4	38) 9/28	39) 6 4/7	40) 34 1/2
41) 4/5	42) 35/36	43) 2 13/40	44) 6
45) 5.1	46) 2.1	47) 1 11/16	48) $157.75
49) 5.26	50) 1.15		

Page 184

1) 996	2) 2,248	3) 3,825	4) 6,972
5) 3,195	6) 62,097	7) 4,408	8) 77,326
9) 704,544	10) 95 R1	11) 204 R8	12) 29 R27
13) 21.3	14) 39.743	15) 25.071	16) $35.08
17) 3.75	18) 4.944	19) 5.36	20) $11.50
21) 19.312	22) 3.4725	23) .21828	24) $744.72
25) .1205	26) .74	27) 16,125	28) $40.71
29) 1 7/45	30) 51/56	31) 9 1/36	32) 14 15/28
33) 30/77	34) 7/24	35) 2 53/78	36) 2 1/2
37) 16/27	38) 7/20	39) 10 3/4	40) 91 2/3
41) 9/20	42) 1/126	43) 3	44) 8/51
45) 3/14	46) 7.45	47) 7 3/11	48) $11.66
49) 21.661	50) 17.84		

Page 185

1) 5.6	2) 13.7	3) 14.69	4) 14.66
5) 418.26	6) 4 1/12	7) 5 7/24	8) 2
9) 1 1/3	10) 2 3/8	11) $7.18	12) 9.05
13) 9,050	14) .0157	15) 10/21	16) 9/25
17) 4 1/8	18) 3.33	19) .00555	20) 1
21) 1 1/4	22) 3/4	23) $23.31	24) $16.29
25) 20.29	26) 19/28	27) 1 7/12	28) 8 5/24
29) $81.53	30) $.11	31) 72.1	32) 60,000
33) $80.91	34) 5 3/7	35) 4 4/7	36) 4
37) 27.41	38) 46.278	39) 6/7	40) 14 11/24
41) 16	42) 30	43) 18	44) 180
45) 120	46) $30.00	47) $3.00	48) $270.00
49) $27.00	50) $237.27		

Page 186

1) 11 1/10	2) 16.3	3) 20.8	4) 70
5) 2/3	6) 5 7/12	7) 105	8) 1 1/2
9) 15.65	10) 3 1/3	11) 3/8	12) 8 11/24
13) 35	14) 6	15) 25.59	16) 30.8
17) 144	18) 1 2/3	19) 1/3	20) 320
21) 2 4/5	22) $23.88	23) .07041	24) 13 2/15
25) 408.26	26).008	27) 3 2/3	28) $970.65
29) 4 4/7	30) 25.3	31) 17.6	32) $.88
33) 97.1	34) 3,750	35) 5 5/6	36) 240
37) 3/28	38) 28 11/18	39) 6 17/20	40) 7.5
41) 39.17	42) .0009	43) $40.71	44) 19/30
45) $12.00	46) $.68	47) 302.13	48) $40,459.78
49) 1 1/6	50) $12.75		

1) 4 3/10	2) 16.5	3) 9.3	4) 5/6
5) 15	6) 9/10	7) 35.42	8) .0015
9) 63	10) 90	11) 45.4	12) 2 3/8
13) 4 7/20	14) 9	15) 218.24	16) 4/9
17) .517	18) 23	19) 7 16/21	20) .10302
21) 3 5/7	22) 33.6	23) 336	24) 1
25) 23.257	26) 26 1/24	27) 64,000	28) 45.23
29) 12 31/40	30) 120	31) 5 5/12	32) 15
33) 7.2	34) 1.932	35) 39 7/18	36) 450
37) 30	38) $.37	39) 470	40) 12 2/5
41) .0004	42) 13 3/5	43) 27	44) 272.976
45) $11.61	46) 2/5	47) .000112	48) .00404
49) 90	50) 1		

1) 13.4	2) 5.3	3) 15.847	4) 22.147
5) 4.44	6) 2.15	7) .02278	8) .00304
9) 500	10) .05	11) 1 7/20	12) 3 17/24
13) 4 4/7	14) 2 3/5	15) 6 13/40	16) 1/6
17) 4	18) 1 1/2	19) 1 1/3	20) 1
21) $16.53	22) $10.27	23) $8.21	24) $12.99
25) $12.90	26) $47.78	27) $5.13	28) $.03
29) $80.13	30) $8.38	31) 13	32) 14
33) 51	34) 1,125	35) 14	36) 65
37) 125,000	38) .0015	39) 140	40) .54
41) 48	42) 4.8	43) 36	44) 180
45) 90	46) 72	47) 270	48) 135
49) $310	50) $329.38		

1) 20.09	2) 7.06	3) 14.5	4) 32.54
5) 13.97	6) 1.36	7) .0156	8) .0206
9) 825	10) 87,500	11) 7 11/15	12) 9 13/24
13) 7 4/9	14) 36 5/8	15) 9	16) 1/9
17) 1 1/2	18) 1 5/9	19) 7 1/2	20) 3
21) $16.56	22) $28.21	23) $19.01	24) $21.00
25) $9.28	26) $2.47	27) $.10	28) $.23
29) $19.55	30) $71.31	31) 15	32) 18
33) 48	34) 60	35) 51	36) 27
37) 108	38) 34	39) 18 2/7	40) 11 2/3
41) 135	42) 288	43) 28.8	44) 875
45) 40	46) 76	47) $98.00	48) 80%
49) 25%	50) 8%		

Page 190

1) 1.87	2) 2.66	3) 19.2	4) 11.567
5) 17.741	6) .0015	7) 7.5	8) .049
9) 44,000	10) .25	11) 7 5/12	12) 3 2/5
13) 6 7/24	14) 4 13/20	15) 2 3/8	16) 1/2
17) 1	18) 5/6	19) 6	20) 32/33
21) $19.46	22) $12.25	23) $.87	24) $6.10
25) $18.06	26) $8.55	27) $279.40	28) $7,125.00
29) $240.08	30) $90.81	31) 30	32) 26
33) 35	34) 57	35) 95	36) 15
37) .015	38) 45,000	39) 7 1/9	40) 400
41) 120	42) 12	43) 1.2	44) 20%
45) 62.5%	46) 125	47) 68	48) $2,205.00
49) $2,327.50	50) $15,000.00		

1) 13.9	2) 6.7	3) 15.5	4) 22.7
5) 6.53	6) .098	7) .00056	8) $25.42
9) .0309	10) 5,000	11) 5 5/8	12) 6 1/4
13) 5 3/4	14) 11 3/14	15) 2 7/24	16) 3/4
17) 5/6	18) 1 1/5	19) 1/8	20) $42.54
21) 16	22) 49	23) 8	24) 729
25) 125	26) 10,000	27) 36	28) 625
29) 3,125	30) 1,024	31) .16	32) .00000081
33) 1.728	34) 1/512	35) 16/625	36) 8
37) 6	38) 9	39) 15	40) 10
41) 33	42) 11	43) 27	44) 18
45) 14	46) 2/3	47) 8/13	48) 1/19
49) .05	50) 1.7		

1) 9	2) 25	3) 27	4) 1,024
5) 4	6) 512	7) 6,561	8) 625
9) 10,000,000	10) 216	11) .09	12) 1.69
13) .00000016	14) 1/16	15) 27/125	16) 3
17) 5	18) 13	19) 12	20) 17
21) 24	22) 26	23) 20	24) 25
25) 31	26) 42	27) .2	28) .14
29) 5/7	30) 1/5	31) 3	32) 5
33) 9	34) 30	35) 24	36) 17
37) 50	38) 26	39) 36	40) 65
41) 65o	42) 82o	43) 60o	44) 60o
45) 60o	46) 40o	47) 100o	48) 80o
49) 122o	50) 35o		

1) −17	2) −7	3) 17	4) 7
5) −7.1	6) 12.6	7) −6 1/4	8) −3.8
9) −.7	10) −4.88	11) 48	12) −.03
13) 300	14) −.0048	15) .03	16) 13 1/2
17) −9/20	18) − 3 1/5	19) 81/500	20) 16/125
21) 6	22) 85	23) 6	24) 105
25) 70	26) 4	27) 1	28) 1.2
29) 9	30) 28	31) 2.7	32) 26,666 2/3
33) 4/5	34) 7,000	35) 72	36) 280
37) 28	38) 36.25	39) 750	40) 25.5
41) 90%	42) 133 1/3%	43) 62.5%	44) 80%
45) 65%	46) 70	47) 292	48) 85
49) 136	50) 34		

1) −15	2) −1	3) 1	4) 15
5) −63	6) −7	7) 5	8) 56
9) −10	10) 20	11) −1 1/2	12) −1 1/2
13) −16 1/2	14) 2 1/4	15) 2.1	16) −.17
17) 500	18) −160	19) −15	20) −2.3
21) 3	22) 8	23) 18	24) 70
25) 34	26) 64	27) 44	28) 57
29) 2 1/4	30) 19 1/2	31) 6/7	32) 3
33) .3125	34) 14	35) 3 5/9	36) 36
37) 21	38) 36	39) 420	40) 42
41) 60%	42) 6%	43) 75%	44) 37 1/2%
45) 80%	46) 25	47) 30	48) 100
49) 24	50) 2,400		

1) 23.4	2) 15.7	3) 11 1/6	4) 24
5) 8/15	6) 6	7) 210	8) 4 4/9
9) .000075	10) 10 2/5	11) 131.4	12) 407.61
13) .0045	14) 31,000	15) $6.72	16) $213.68
17) 51.65	18) 5 15/28	19) 34	20) 14 3/8
21) 3	22) −13	23) −3	24) 40
25) −40	26) −3	27) 3	28) 63
29) −9	30) −336	31) −1 1/8	32) 5 1/5
33) 27	34) 11/12	35) 2/3	36) 1.5
37) 1,000	38) 24.8	39) .54	40) −6.16
41) −48	42) 43	43) −8	44) 15
45) −11	46) 136	47) −10	48) −250
49) −30	50) −79		

1) 77	2) −77	3) −91	4) 91
5) −588	6) 588	7) −12	8) 12
9) 7.1	10) 17	11) −15.2	12) −7.39
13) −.13	14) −2.08	15) 13,000	16) −.208
17) −7 1/2	18) 10 1/2	19) −10 1/2	20) 8 1/2
21) −27	22) 48	23) −27	24) −3 1/5
25) 1/25	26) 25	27) 22	28) −29
29) −261	30) 11	31) 6	32) −3
33) 4	34) −7	35) −3	36) 5
37) 5	38) −17	39) 9	40) 21
41) −84	42) 20	43) −1.95	44) 800
45) −.02	46) −4	47) −706	48) .0005
49) 50	50) 16,500		

1) −30	2) −18	3) 18	4) 30
5) −17 3/4	6) 17 3/4	7) −17.7	8) 3.9
9) 6.06	10) 6.54	11) −1.44	12) .0144
13) −1.44	14) −4	15) .04	16) −4,000
17) 400	18) −12	19) 15	20) 15/32
21) −1 1/5	22) −2/5	23) −4 4/5	24) 4 4/5
25) −7.95	26) 9	27) 46	28) −9
29) 28	30) −28	31) 48	32) 13
33) −19	34) −11	35) 7	36) 18
37) 24	38) 33	39) −24	40) −11
41) 7	42) 10 1/2	43) 4 1/2	44) 5
45) 5	46) 15	47) 48.48	48) 130
49) 108	50) .07		

1) 12	2) −18	3) −12	4) 18
5) −45	6) 45	7) −5	8) 5
9) −12.7	10) −3.3	11) −1 1/5	12) 8
13) −2 11/15	14) 7 5/21	15) .06	16) −.015
17) −1,500	18) −5.5	19) 3.9	20) −1 1/2
21) −1	22) −.3	23) −170,000	24) −11.44
25) 6.85	26) 16	27) −1 5/12	28) −5.3
29) 22 1/2	30) 24	31) −.09	32) 70
33) −17/40	34) 4	35) −7	36) −1/4
37) 9	38) −54	39) 18	40) 7 1/2
41) −49	42) 5	43) 19	44) −12 1/2
45) −17	46) −19.8	47) 40	48) 14
49) 300	50) 8		

Page 199

1) 17.5

2) 9.4

3) 54.717

4) .252

5) $3.72

6) .02

7) 20

8) 24 2/15

9) 4 2/5

10) 9 7/24

11) 2/3

12) 27/32

13) 1 1/12

14) 60

15) 6

16) 60%

17) 70

18) $637.50

19) 5

20) 5

21) −21

22) −3

23) −7/8

24) −13 23/24

25) −2 7/8

26) 36

27) −36

28) −36

29) −14

30) 14

31) −14

32) 1 1/2

33) 6

34) 156

35) 210

36) −31

37) −4.02

38) −7

39) 2 1/2

40) −.04

41) A > −2

42) B ≤ 2

43) 112 sq. ft.; 44 ft.

44) 169 sq. in.; 52 in.

45) 160 sq. cm; 67 cm

46) 150 sq. m; 60m

47) 1,000 sq.in.; 140 in.

48) 375 sq. cm; 94 cm

49) 2,826 sq.m; 188.4 m

50) 616 sq. ft.; 88 ft.

Page 200

1) −2

2) −16

3) −2

4) 2

5) −14/15

6) −13.875

7) −10.17

8) −9.6

9) 96

10) −12

11) −16

12) 54

13) −8

14) 15,000

15) −14.85

16) 45

17) −6

18) 23

19) −9

20) −.06

21) −13.5

22) 5

23) 109.2

24) 48

25) −.02

26) 72

27) 20

28) 40%

29) 52

30) $1,350.00

31) $1,000.00

32) $1,125.00

33) $630.00

34) $1,500.00

35) $7.50; $22.50

36) $1,900.00; $7,600.00

37) $101.25; $573.75

38) 9

39) 64

40) 6.25

41) 625   42) 8   43) 24   44) 90 ft.;
                                                    500 sq. ft.

45) 18 cm;   46) 84 in.;   47) 160 m;   48) 195 ft.;
    204 1/4 sq.cm   294 sq. in.   1,200 sq. m   1,500 sq. ft.

49) 628 cm;   50) 132 in.;
    31,400 sq.cm   1,386 sq. in.

PRACTICE   PRACTICE   PRACTICE

BOOK I

Whole Numbers	Prime Numbers
Rounding	GCF
Decimals	LCM
Money	Fractions

33 Review and combination pages

BOOK II

Percents	Exponents
Integers	Estimation
Rationals	Scientific Notation
Equations	Evaluating Expressions
Inequalities	Order of Operations
Probability	Geometry
Perimeter	Volume
Area	Surface Area

for more information contact
ST² PUBLISHING
203 SI TOWN RD.
CASTLE ROCK, WA 98611
360-636-2645 TEL
360-414-5243 FAX
WEB SITE: http://kalama.com/~st2pub
EMAIL: st2pub@kalama.com

PAGE 201

1. 2/24 = N/36, 3 HOURS
3. 3/8 = N/192, 72 STRIKEOUTS
5. 1/36 = N/432, 12 GALLONS
7. 1/5 = N/15, 3 WINS, 12 LOSSES
9. 3/183 = N/1098, 18 HOURS
11. 1 1/2/64 = N/192, 4 1/2 LBS.
13. 28/8 = N/12, 42 TOUCHDOWNS

2. 3/48 = 5/N, 80 CAKES
4. 4/18 = N/108, 24 LOST BALLS
6. 45/4 = 30/N, 2 2/3 MILES
8. 3/1440 = 5/N, 2400 STEAKS
10. 6/150 = N/200, 8 LBS.
12. 4/6 = 10/N, 15 HOURS

PAGE 202

1. 3/8 = N/32, 12 HOMERUNS
3. 24/1 = 528/N, 22 GAMES
5. 45/6 = N/20, 150 LBS.
7. 3/1.8 = N/240, 400 GALLONS
9. 108/5 = N/60, 1296 WORDS
   1296/1 = N/1 1/2, 1944 WORDS
   1296/1 = N/8, 10,368 WORDS

2. 24/16 = 72/N, 48 SHIRTS
4. 455/6 1/2 = 2100/N, 30 HOURS
6. 4/27 = N/108, 16 BIRDIES
8. 30.6/1 = N/15, 459 MILES
   459/1 = 2295/N, 5 TANKS
10. 1 1/2/6 = N/16, 4 LBS.

11. 288/30 = 8640/N, 900 LBS, 1.5/1 = 900/N, 600 CANS
12. HOME 3/4 = N/20, AWAY 2/5 = N/15: 1. 15 WINS   2. 6 WINS
    3. 21 WINS   4. 14 LOSSES   5. 75% HOME   6. 40% AWAY   7. 60% TOTAL

PAGE 203

1. 7/8 = N/100, 87.5%
3. 6/N = 40/100, 15 CATS
5. 160/120 = N/100, 133 1/3%

7. 28/N = 13 1/3/100, 210 LBS.

9. N/16 = 12 1/2/100, 2 HOURS
11. N/32 = 75/100, 24 NOT MISSING
    ASSIGNMENTS, 8 MISSING SOME
13. 12/200 = N/100, 28/200 = N/100,
    1. 6% 2. 14% 3. 20%

2. N/25 = 68/100, 17 STRIKEOUTS
4. N/50 = 94/100, 3 MISSED PROBLEMS
6. N/1,500,000,000 = 3/100,
   45,000,000 BACTERIA
8. N/84 = 40/100, 34 PUTTS
   50/N = 40/100, 125 SHOTS
10. 48/60 = N/100, 80% SUCCESS,
    20% MISSED
12. 18/N = 8/100, 1. 207 RIGHT. 2.
    213.75 RIGHT. 3. 11.25 MISSED.
    4. 225 PROBLEMS

1. 66,5ØØ/7Ø,ØØØ = N/1ØØ,
   95% FULL, 3,5ØØ EMPTY SEATS
3. $294/N = 7Ø/1ØØ, $42Ø LIST
   PRICE, $126 SAVED
5. 3Ø/75 = N/1ØØ, 4Ø% PUTTS,
   15/75 = N/1ØØ, 2Ø% DRIVES
7. N/25 = 2Ø/1ØØ, 5 MILES SAVED,
   2Ø MILES ON I-5

9. 32/N = 8Ø/1ØØ, 4Ø PROBLEMS,
   8 MISSED
11. N/$9ØØ = 65/1ØØ, $315 PAYED,
    $585 SAVED

2. N/45 = 8Ø/1ØØ, 36A'S, 9B'S
4. N/97Ø = 3Ø/1ØØ, 291 MOUNTAINOUS
   MILES, 679 NON-MOUNTAINOUS
   MILES
6. N/$8ØØ = 4Ø/1ØØ, $32Ø SAVED,
   $48Ø PAID
8. 135/N = 75/1ØØ, 1. 18Ø PRE-
   DICTIONS. 2. 45 WINS
   3. 45/18Ø = N/1ØØ, 25% WINS
10. 35/N = 7Ø/1ØØ, 5Ø TIES, 15
    DECENT TIES
12. 27/N = 45/1ØØ, 6Ø% FREE THROWS
    SHOT, 33 MISSED

1. N/42Ø = 6Ø/1ØØ, 252 COMPLETE,
   168 INCOMPLETE
3. 27/N = 6Ø/1ØØ, 45 SPLITS,
   18 NOT PICKED UP
5. 18/N = 3Ø/1ØØ, 6Ø FACULTY
   MEMBERS, 42 NON-COUGAR FANS
7. N/4Ø = 15Ø/1ØØ, PAT 6Ø SHIRTS,
   2Ø MORE SHIRTS
9. 27/9Ø = N/1ØØ, 3Ø% ABSENT,
   63 TIMES PRESENT

2. $6Ø/$3ØØ = N/1ØØ, 2Ø% SAVED,
   $24Ø PAYED
4. N/65Ø = 35/1ØØ, 1. 65% 2.
   422.5 MILES, 3. 227.5 MILES
6. 259/37Ø = N/1ØØ, 1. TERRI
   7Ø%, 2. STEVE 3Ø%
8. N/$12ØØ = 4Ø/1ØØ, $72Ø PAYED,
   $48Ø SAVED
10. 3/12 = N/1ØØ, 25% GOOD, 75% BAD,
    3Ø GOOD JOKES, 9Ø BAD JOKES

11. RONNIE T. N/2ØØ = 3Ø/1ØØ, 26Ø YDS.; TEEVEE N/26Ø = 9Ø/1ØØ, 234 YDS.;
    GOOSEE N/2ØØ = 2Ø/1ØØ 24Ø YDS.; GLENDA N/2ØØ = 8Ø/1ØØ, 16Ø YDS.;
    KATHY N/16Ø = 15/1ØØ, 184 YDS.

1. 411 LOST FRIENDS
3. 85% CORRECT
5. 6/$1.44 = 8/N, $1.92, $3.36 TOTAL
7. TOTAL 34.6 YDS., AVE. 5.8 YDS.
9. DOWN $4,3ØØ, SALES TAX $15Ø5,
   LICENSE $45Ø, TOTAL $6255
11. 1Ø/3 = N/24, 8Ø LIMES

2. 84,ØØØ LBS. OF WHEAT
4. 395 YARDS
6. BOTH - 7.2 QTS., SMALL -
   3.1 QTS., LARGE 4.1 QTS.
8. $152
10. 5 HOURS 3Ø MIN., 6 HR.
    3Ø MIN., 4 HR. 3Ø MIN.,
    5 HR., 8 HR. 45 MIN.

1. 103 GALLONS
2. $8.75 A MONTH, $105 A YEAR
3. $379.75
4. $1.60 A RIDE
5. 108 BOOKS
6. $510 IN 1989, $909 TOTAL
7. 1. STEAK $42.96, POTATO SALAD $6.84, CORN $2.33, LEMONADE $5, TOTAL $57.13
   2. 24/$57.13 = 6/N, $14.28, $71.41
8. TIM 74, CHET 90, ED 76, MIKE 75, DAMIAN 82, DON 80, KEN 77, THE GAPP 94

1. 1. 61.7 IN. 2. 59.3 IN. 3. 20.7 IN. 4. 22.5 IN. 5. 42.3 IN.
   6. 58. IN 7. 27.3 IN. 8. 56.7 IN. 9. 41.6 IN.
2. 1. 38.7 IN. 2. 38 IN. 3. 22.3 IN. 4. 24 IN. 5. 32.8 IN.
   6. 35.8 IN. 7. 26 IN. 8. 34.7 IN. 9. 31.4 IN.

3.

	A.	B.
BLOUSE	$13.50	$9.00
SKIRT	$12.50	$15.00
SHOES	$36.00	$27.00
SWEATER	$37.91	$26.76
COAT	$62.00	$55.80
STOCKINGS	$25.20	$21.60
JEANS	$19.47	$17.97
TOTAL	$206.58	$173.13
SALES TAX	$ 14.46	$ 13.85
TOTAL BILL	$221.04	$186.98
INTEREST	$ 3.17	$ 2.65
TOTAL	$224.21	$189.63

4. 1. $ .48
   2. $ 2.88
   3. $ 7.20
   4. $ .72
   5. $ .96
   6. $ 2.16
   7. $ 4.32
   8. $17.28
   9. $120.00

1. 1. 75Ø SQ. FT.,   2. 2 1/2 OR
        3 GALLONS
3. FRONT - 75Ø SQ. FT., SIDE 25Ø
    SQ. FT., BACK 1ØØØ SQ. FT.,
    5 CANS OF MOSQUITO SPRAY.
5. 357 HOT DOGS
7. 1. 26 MILES ON SURFACE STREETS
        78 MILES ON FREEWAYS
    2. 3Ø MINUTES ON SURFACE STREETS
        72 MINUTES ON FREEWAYS, 1Ø2
        MIN. (1 HR. 42 MIN.) TOTAL

2. 1. 168 SQ. FT., 2. 8Ø
    SQ. FT., 3. 3ØØ SQ. FT.
4. 3.7 OR 4 CANS
4. 39 BIDS MADE
6. 1. 15,ØØØ PRIZES, 2. 45,ØØØ
    PRIZES, 3. 13,5ØØ PRIZES,
    4. 31,5ØØ PRIZES
8. 1. 89.7   2. 96.7
    3. 8Ø.3   4. 91.5
9. 1. 21.7   2. 14.3 3. 15.8
    4. 27.7   5. 27   6. 22.8
    7. 21

1. STANFORD 18, UCLA 24, ARIZONA ST. 16, OREGON ST. 21, WASHINGTON 17,
    OREGON 19, WASHINGTON ST. 2Ø, CALIFORNIA 16, ARIZONA 19, USC 1Ø.

2. SEATTLE 96, MINNESOTA 9Ø, CHICAGO 75, TEXAS 65, OAKLAND 48, KANSAS
    CITY 86, CALIFORNIA 9Ø, MILWAUKEE 6Ø, BOSTON 75, DETROIT 75,
    BALTIMORE 6Ø, CLEVELAND 8Ø, TORONTO 9Ø, NEW YORK 74.

3. GREGORI $12Ø.ØØ, LENA $6Ø.ØØ, ANNA $9Ø.ØØ, NICHOLAS $15Ø.ØØ,
    MILO $18Ø.ØØ.

4. JOSE $468.ØØ, RONALDO $288.ØØ, LUIGI $144.ØØ, CARMELA $18Ø.ØØ,
    JUAN $36Ø.ØØ.

5.
	QUARTERS	DIMES	NICKELS	-	QT.	DIMES-NICK.	-	QT.	DIMES-NICK.
1.	6	1	8	-	5	5 5	-	4	9 2
2.	7	4	9	-	6	8 6	-	5	12 3
3.	9	2	14	-	8	6 11	-	7	1Ø 8
	6	14	5	-	5	18 2			
4.	6	4	16	-	5	8 13	-	4	12 1Ø
	3	16	7	-	2	2Ø 4	-	1	24 1

6. 1. 21,22,23; 2. 21,23,25; 3. 32,34,36; 4. 15,2Ø,25;
    5. 28,42,56; 6. 52,65,78,91,1Ø4; 7. 4,4 1/2,5;
    8. 4.5,6,7.5,9,1Ø.5;   9. $1.25,$1.5Ø,$1.75,$2.ØØ,$2.25
    1Ø. $3.75, $5.ØØ, $6.25, $7.5Ø, $8.75;

1. $20,21,22$; $N+N+1+N+2=63$
2. $19,21,23$; $N+N+2+N+4=63$
3. $18,20,22$; $N+N+2+N+4=60$
4. $15,20,25$; $N+N+5+N+10=60$
5. $72,73$; $N+N+1=145$
6. $34,35,36$; $N+N+1+N+2=105$
7. $56,58$; $N+N+2=114$
8. $31,33,35$; $N+N+2+N+4=99$
9. $29,31,33$; $N+N+4=62$
10. $-13,-12,-11$, $N+N+1=3(N+2)+8$
11. $3,5,7$; $8N=3(N+4)+3$
12. $12,14,16,18$;
13. $4,5,6,7$;
$$N+N+2+N+4=N+6+24$$
$$N+N+3=4(N+1)\ -9$$
14. $6,8,10$; $5(N+2)+3(N+4)=70$
15. $N=6$; $5N+8=8N-10$
16. $N=3$; $25-4N=N+10$
17. $33,22$; $N+N-11=55$
18. $7,25$; $32-N=3N+4$
19. $-1,-3$; $N+5=N/3+3$

1. $L=20$ IN., $W=16$ IN.,
$2W + 2W + 8 = 72$
2. $W=6$ CM, $L=14$ CM.
$2W + 4W + 4 = 40$
3. $W=12$ IN., $L=42$ IN.
$2W + 7W = 108$
4. $L=23$ CM, $W=19$ CM
$2L + 2L - 8 = 84$
5. $W=50$ M, $L=110$ M
$2W + 4W + 20 = 320$
6. $W=28$ FT., $L(72-W)=44$ FT.
$3W = 2(72-W) - 4$
7. HELEN $= 3N = 15$ YEARS
MILLIE $= N = 5$ YEARS
$2(N + 5) = 3N + 5$
8. CHAN $= 4N = 16$ YEARS
COUSIN $= N = 4$ YEARS
$4N + 8 = 2(N + 8)$
9. MR. GOMEZ $= N + 25 = 46$ YEARS
MR. KOWALSKI $= N = 21$ YEARS
$N + 4 = 1/2(N + 25 + 4)$
10. 8 YEARS AGO
$24 - N = 4(12 - N)$
11. GREG $= N = 16$ YEARS
SHERRI $= 42 - N = 26$ YEARS
$N + 14 = 2(42 - N - 11)$
12. GIRLS $= N = 10$
BOYS $= N + 9 = 19$
$N + N + 9 = 29$
13. ASHLEY $= N = 9$; JILL $= 5N = 45$;
MARIA $= N + 4 = 13$ TICKETS
$5N + N + N + 4 = 67$
14. PACO $= 3N + 4 = 127$ LBS.
BROTHER $= N = 41$ LBS.
$3N + 4 + N = 168$
15. JOSH $= N = 220$ CARDS
BORIS $= 1/2N + 30 = 140$ CARDS
$N + 1/2N + 30 = 360$

1. QUARTERS = N = 7
    DIMES = N - 3 = 4
    .1(N - 3) + .25N = $2.15
3. NICKELS = N = 2
    DIMES = 3N = 6
    QUARTERS = 2N = 4
    .05N +.1(3N)+.25(2N)=$1.70
5. NICKELS = N = 18
    DIMES = N - 12 = 6
    QUARTERS = N - 6 = 12
    .05N + .1(N-12) +.25(N-6)=$4.50
7. UNITS = N - 4 = 1
    TENS = N = 5
    10N + N-4 = 9(N + N-4) - 3
9. $.80 = N = 20 LBS.
    $.65 = 60 - N = 40 LBS.
    .80N + .65(60 - N) = 60(.70)
11. ADULT = N = 121
    STUDENT = 420 - N = 299
    4N + 2.5(420 - N) = $1231.50

13. N = NUMBER OF HOURS = 3.5
    600 MPH JET = 600N = 2100 MILES
    750 MPH JET = 750N = 2625 MILES
    600N + 750N = 4725

2. NICKELS = N = 24
    DIMES = 48 - N = 24
    .05N + .1(48 - N) = $3.60
4. ONE DOLLAR BILLS = N = 9
    FIVE DOLLAR BILLS = 2N = 18
    TEN DOLLAR BILLS = 1/3N = 3
    N+(5 X 2N)+(10 X 1/3N)=$129
6. UNITS = N + 6 = 9
    TENS = N = 3
    10N + N + 6 = 3(N+N+6) + 3
8. UNITS = N = 2
    TENS = N + 5 = 7
    N + N + 5 = 9
10. $1.40 = 45 - N = 15 LBS.
    $1.25 = N = 30 LBS.
    1.40(45 - N) +1.25N = 45(1.30)
12. N = NUMBER OF HOURS
    S.A. TO DALLAS=50N= 150 MILES
    DALLAS TO S.A.=40N= 120 MILES
    50N + 40N = 270
    N = 3 HOURS

PRACTICE PRACTICE PRACTICE

BOOK I

WHOLE NUMBERS	PRIME NUMBERS
ROUNDING	GCF
DECIMALS	LCM
MONEY	FRACTIONS

33 REVIEW AND COMBINATION PAGES

BOOK II

PERCENTS	EXPONENTS
INTEGERS	ESTIMATION
RATIONALS	SCIENTIFIC NOTATION
EQUATIONS	EVALUATION EXPRESSIONS
INEQUALITIES	ORDER OF OPERATIONS
PROBABILITY	GEOMETRY
PERIMETER	VOLUME
AREA	SURFACE AREA

PROBLEM SOLVING
  A. SHORT ANSWERS
  B. MULTIPLE ANSWERS
  C. ALGEBRA EQUATIONS

FOR MORE INFORMATION CONTACT

2

ST PUBLISHING
2Ø3 SI TOWN ROAD
CASTLE ROCK, WA 98611
360-636-2645 TEL
360-414-5243 FAX
WEB SITE: http://kalama.com/~st2pub
EMAIL: st2pub@kalama.com